Carolyn Badger, PhD., Psychologist
"This gem of a book is obviously written by standing of the subject. It is a 'how to' book on the profound emotions that are part of this journey. Every divorcing couple should read it!"

Jeff Zimmerman, Ph.D., ABPP, co-author of *The Co-Parenting Survival Guide*
"In this easy to read book Vikki tells you (like she is speaking to you in person) what, when, where, how and how much to tell your children about the major change in the family called 'divorce'. She gives you tips about managing your own emotions, keeping the children out of the conflict and being attuned with your children. In short, this book can help parents be their best selves as they help their children during this difficult time."

Adele Faber, co-author of *How to Talk So Kids Will Listen & Listen So Kids Will Talk*
"A rich, loving, and deeply comforting guide to parents determined to steer their children safely through the trauma of divorce."

Elizabeth S. Thayer, Ph.D., co-author of *The Co-Parenting Survival Guide*
"This is a much needed and complete discussion of one of the most difficult moments between parents and children as families reconfigure during a divorce. It gives a realistic picture of the complicated emotions of both children and parents and also clear steps for preparation before, during, and after the initial talk. This book provides parents and professionals with an additional tool for helping children successfully move into their new lives truly feeling heard, loved and cared by both of their parents."

Jessica G. Lippman, Ph.D., co-author of *Divorcing With Children* and *Helping Children Cope With the Death of a Parent*
"Vikki Stark has written a book that will be genuinely helpful to those seeking answers on how and when to tell the children the painful information that the family they know will no longer exist. She has an informal and personally driven approach that is accessible to the reader. *The Divorce Talk: How to Tell the Kids* is a helpful, practical guide that steers parents through this murky area by providing actual scripts so that the children will be helped through the telling relatively unscathed."

This book is an original production of Green Light Press
Montreal, Quebec
Canada

For information, contact:
Green Light Press
books@greenlight-press.com

Please Visit: www.HowToTellTheKids.com

Library and Archives Canada Cataloguing in Publication

Stark, Vikki, author
        The divorce talk : how to tell the kids : a parent's guide
to breaking the news without breaking their hearts / Vikki Stark.

Title of previous edition: Divorce : how to tell the kids.
Includes bibliographical references.
Issued in print and electronic formats.
ISBN 978-0-9864721-5-2 (paperback).–ISBN 978-0-9864721-6-9 (html)

1. Children of divorced parents. 2. Divorce. 3. Child rearing.
I. Title.

HQ777.5.S723 2016   306.89   C2015-907081-3
                                       C2015-907082-1

Cover photo by Paul Edmondson

The
DIVORCE TALK
How to Tell the Kids

A Parent's Guide to Breaking the News
without Breaking Their Hearts

VIKKI STARK

For Adrian

Contents

Other books by Vikki Stark

*My Sister, My Self: The Surprising Ways That Being an Older,
Middle, Younger or Twin Shaped Your Life*

*Runaway Husbands: The Abandoned Wife's Guide
to Recovery and Renewal*

Acknowledgements

There are few moments in life universally seen as turning points. Learning that your parents are getting divorced while you are still a child or teen is certainly one of them. For many that discussion gets lost in the myriad changes that result from it and rarely gets revisited.

When asked about it later, people have strong feelings about how it was handled in their lives. If it was handled well, they want to proudly state it. If it was handled poorly, they want that fact acknowledged. Either way, many people feel passionately that they want to reduce the suffering of other children in the future who face this juncture.

My deep appreciation goes to the boys and girls, teens, and men and women who participated in the study that led to this book. I know that going back over that territory stirred things up for you, yet you persevered. It is through understanding your reality that I was able to fully grasp the many nuances of experience at this sensitive time. I hope that your wish, to reduce the suffering of other children, is realized as a result.

Many wonderful friends supported me in this project but I want to give special thanks to Jeanette Limondjian and Andrea McElhone, who walked with me every step of the way. My daughters, Lauren and Michele Goldman, proved invaluable sounding boards for my thoughts and ideas—they encouraged some and helped me wisely discard others. Michele used her phenomenal talent to create the beautiful website for the book, www.HowToTellTheKids.com.

It's a rare privilege to have someone who cares about your project as much as you do and I have been lucky enough to have that with Adrian Zimmermann. His wisdom, vision and project management skills helped me structure this work from its beginning in 2011 and navigate through its many phases to realization.

The
DIVORCE TALK

How to Tell the Kids

CHAPTER I

A Bridge to Your New Life

Jennifer was deep in thought as she sat on the back deck cradling a mug of coffee, watching the kids play in the yard. Hannah, ten, was intent on capturing the snails that were clinging to the grass after last night's rain. Tyler, seven, was patiently attempting to launch the remote control thingamajig he'd gotten for his birthday last week.

In their own worlds, the kids had no idea that their lives were about to change in a way that Jennifer dreaded with all her heart. When Michael, her husband of fifteen years, comes home from work, they will finally tell the kids that they are getting divorced. She'd agonized over the decision for months, trying to find some other alternative, but every road led to the same dead end. The marriage was over and the kids needed to know.

Jennifer was sick with worry; everything about the future was unknown, starting with how this conversation would go. She wasn't sure that Michael would stick with the plan and not blame her or tell the kids the things she'd asked him to keep private. What if the discussion deteriorated into a shouting match? What if they said awful things? What if she cried or, worse, he cried? How could they protect their precious, innocent children when the feelings between them were so raw?

Telling your children that you're getting separated or divorced is rough. Some parents say that it's the hardest thing they've ever had to do. You worry terribly about how it will affect your child, both today and in the long run. You worry that your children will be deeply upset or angry. And most of all, you worry that you won't know how to help.

To make it even tougher, *the divorce talk* comes at a time in your own life when you're struggling. If you're the one being left, you may be in shock and grieving. If you're the one who made the decision to leave, you may feel guilty and deeply burdened. This is often the point at which parents seek out a family therapist like myself for that one anguished session—the *How do we tell the kids?* session.

Over the years, I've met with countless separating couples who desperately wanted to know how to do it right. They would anxiously ask:

- "Should we tell them before they leave for camp or when they come back, right before school?"
- "I need to tell my daughter that I'm not to blame! Is that a bad idea?"
- "Don't they need to know about the affair? I can't lie!"
- "He's already a nervous kid! What is this going to do to him?"

There are many, many questions that parents need to answer in order to make *the divorce talk* as smooth as possible. Many people believe that having divorced parents is always destructive for children—I don't agree. It's usually not the mere fact of divorce that causes the greatest harm. Rather, it's the ongoing conflict that does the most damage.

Psychologists Peter A. Levine and Maggie Kline, authors of *Trauma-Proofing Your Kids*, wrote: "Grief is unavoidable but trauma is preventable!" That's my purpose in writing this book. I want to teach you the attuned response—listening carefully, acknowledging and accepting your children's feelings—which will contribute to making *the divorce talk* as nontraumatic as possible. By providing you with all the information you need on every facet of *the divorce talk* and helping you get in touch with your strongest, most balanced self, this book will aid you in crafting the best way to break the news to your kids about your upcoming separation.

That's not to say that your children will not be tearful, angry, or hurt—those are normal, expected emotions. But in spite of those feelings, because you will have learned to be attuned to their emotions, you *will* know what to do to help. You won't eliminate the grief, but you will learn how to reduce the threat of trauma.

Becoming Attuned to Your Child's Emotions

Attunement is key. That means being able to correctly identify and acknowledge what your child is feeling without trying to change it. Children find it profoundly comforting to know that they have a parent who really understands and accepts their feelings, particularly when something scary and unwanted is taking place. It is extremely important for children to feel that they are not alone with their emotions. Not being in tune with their children's emotions at this pivotal moment in their lives is one of the biggest mistakes parents can make. Psychologist Anthony Wolf wrote:

> If divorce and its consequences cause kids to suffer, how can parents help their children deal with that suffering? What can parents do so that the suffering doesn't turn into damage? You cannot *undo* the true bad that comes into your children's lives. You cannot, with just the right words, with just the right acts of deep love and caring, make it all better. Bad feelings from bad things are real and cannot be washed away. But they can be shared, which in the end is the best way for you to help your children put their bad feelings to rest. In doing so, they do not feel so alone. Be with them and let them know you care.

He's right. You can't make it not hurt. But once you learn how to be attuned to your child's needs, you can soften the blow and help turn this experience into a lesson about how to face hard things in life. Our kids are tender travelers in a tough world, but your courage and wisdom can help ease their journey.

So what's our ideal scenario for Jennifer and Michael? In a perfect world, they would have discussed what to tell the kids about why they are separating and what will be happening next in their lives. With kids the ages of Hannah and Tyler, they shouldn't go into too much detail during the revelation. They would know who speaks first and how much to say—and they would not deviate much from that plan. Jennifer and Michael may be sad and there may be tears, but that's okay because they will demonstrate that in spite of their grief, they are still the parents and still in charge.

Their demeanor will be mature and civil, and neither will use *the divorce talk* to score points. Most of all, they will be *attuned* to their children's reactions—listening carefully, acknowledging, and accepting. And this first step toward their new life, as painful as it may be, will be handled with an awareness that it sets the stage for how well their precious children will do with the changes to come. And, in that perfect world, when *the divorce talk* is over, they will feel proud of how they handled it.

Seven Steps for Breaking the News without Breaking Their Hearts

Jennifer and Michael's ideal scenario may not be possible for you, but there is much to learn from aiming high! What tools do *you* need to be able to successfully accomplish this crucial parenting task of telling *your* kids in the best way possible?

The Seven Steps for Breaking the News

1 Learn to manage your own emotions so you will be in the best shape possible when you talk to your children.

2 If you can, have a planning meeting with your spouse to work out the basics of what you are going to tell the kids.

3 Understand the meaning of the divorce for your particular kids.

4 Decide who should do the telling, where and when to tell, and what to say to explain why you are getting separated. If you cannot work effectively with your spouse, decide these things yourself.

5 Tell your kids that you are getting separated.

6 Using the art of being attuned to your children's emotions—listening carefully, acknowledging and accepting—respond appropriately to their reactions thereby reducing the risk of trauma.

7 Follow through using suggested strategies so you can remain attuned in the days and weeks following *the divorce talk*.

Mastering these *Seven Steps* will ensure that you have done everything you can to make this transition in your children's lives as smooth as possible. There are no guarantees that you won't go through a rough period while you and your children are adjusting to the new reality—you probably will—but at least you will know how to deal with this challenge and recognize that the turmoil will likely settle down in time.

Psychologist Joan B. Kelly wrote, "Parents need help in understanding that telling the children about the divorce provides a signal opportunity to help the child cope with the crisis, and that the telling is not an act apart but a central component in the supportive role of the parent."

The time and thought you put into the revelation of your up-coming separation will set the stage for how your children deal with this change in the future. You're creating a bridge between your old life as a married family living together and your new one, perhaps as a binuclear family with two homes. The waters below the bridge may be turbulent, the sky above may be filled with clouds, but there is no way around it—you have to go over it to reach your new life and stability on the other side. I know you can do it. I'll help you!

Why am I uniquely qualified to guide you across? First, I have over thirty years' experience as a marriage counselor, family ther-apist, and divorce recovery specialist. Second, in order to really understand what children experience when they learn that their parents are separating, I conducted over a hundred interviews with children and with adults who were children when their par-ents divorced. This enabled me to deeply connect with the real-ity of those going through it. Third, I also interviewed parents who had already done *the divorce talk* who, from the wisdom of hindsight, could evaluate what they did well or what they wish they had done differently. Finally, I researched and learned from everything written on the subject by other professionals in the field of children and divorce.

Hearing from the Kids and Parents Who Participated in the Study

Throughout the book, you'll be hearing the experiences and ad-vice of kids and parents who have already lived it. I learned from the participants two ways. Either I interviewed them face-to-face or they completed an online questionnaire. Some younger chil-dren worked on the questionnaire with a parent. When I quote the participants throughout the book, the age next to their name represents their age at the time of their parents' separation.

These kids will tell you what was important to them when they heard about their parents' divorce—what helped or hurt, and what advice they have for you. This will help you understand what it feels like to receive the news and what children really want to know when they do. It's like reading a letter from your own child, telling you what he needs!

One of the questions I asked the kids was, "Did your parents say or do anything that made you feel better?" The answers were so simple. Kids wanted hugs and the reassurance that it wasn't their fault. Here are some of their responses:

- Maggie, who was 3 when her parents separated: "My mom was very attentive and just held me until I felt better."
- Kerry, 10: "Lots of hugging and holding us."
- Hilary, 9: "At the time I would have said that all of their reassurances made me feel better."
- Benny, 6: "Hugs & kisses/listening to my sadness."
- Daryl, 9: "My parents explained that there wasn't going to be too much of a change, that we would still see each other. That made me feel better. Also being told I was loved."
- Chloe, 12: "They assured my brother and me that it wasn't our fault."
- Athena, 11: "Not much conversation, but I still remember the words 'I love you.'"
- Ian, 13: "Them saying, 'It wasn't your fault.'"

Most eloquently, Sophie, who was eleven when she participated in the study but just eight years old when her parents divorced, had some specific suggestions about how to go about *the divorce talk*, "Go on vacation and don't tell him/her when they're playing their favorite game. If the kid is young, don't bring them to a therapist because he/she is only going to want to play the games and not talk. Anyway it's better to leave your kid in school. P.s., I'm not kidding!"

You'll also hear from parents who have already broken the news to their kids and learn what they did that they feel most proud of—and what they regret. Here are some answers to the question, "What did you do that you're most proud of?"

- Jude: "I didn't say *anything* that I regretted in front of my son or to his father. I act respectfully toward my son's father. I tell my son I want them to have a relationship and that I'll be OK and that he can meet the woman his father is with and I won't think he's being disloyal to me. I have tried to make it easier for my son even if I have to hide how I really feel."
- Carmela: "I did not cry and instead I tried to portray a strong woman who knows her mind."
- Dave: "I always told my daughter (10) it's going to be OK. It may not look like it now, but it will eventually. I also told her that as long as we kept communication open between us, we would be fine. It was OK to not want to talk all the time, but that we couldn't not talk and hope that everything would just go away."
- Edith: "I'm happy that I could reassure my boys that it was not their fault, that although it was devastating we would survive it. I'm proud that I did not scream and shout at my ex-husband in front of my boys."
- Betsy-Ann: "I stood by my children through everything and kept everything as open as possible for them. I allowed them to ask questions and gave them honest responses. We are so close now. We are the three stooges! We have so much fun and they are my world. I have encouraged as much contact with their dad as the kids want."
- Carly: "I took time in myself to collect my thoughts and understand my feelings."
- Angela: "I think going through the grief together made us stronger. In fact, we still have times of sadness and grief and we get though them together. We call them 'sad days.'"
- And Clark wryly wrote: "I didn't shoot myself, so that was a plus."

I've also culled words of wisdom from other therapists and researchers who have explored this question. We've got all the bases covered to prepare you as completely as possible.

A note of housekeeping: in the interest of smooth communication, I will randomly be referring to "your children" or "your child" and alternate using "he" and "she." The names of the participants in the study on which this book is based have been changed to protect their privacy, although all quotes used are verbatim.

Let's get started!

TAKEAWAY from *A Bridge to Your New Life*

- You cannot avoid the anger or grief your child may feel when she learns about your separation, but you can learn skills to reduce the risk of trauma.
- Becoming attuned to your child's emotions will help him feel that he's not alone. Attunement means listening carefully, acknowledging and accepting your child's feelings.
- Hearing the actual words of children who have experienced parental separation will sensitize you to what your own child needs.
- Advice from parents who have gone through what you are going through will encourage and inform you.

CHAPTER 2

Understanding Your Own Emotions

It was incomprehensible to Trevor how much Aisha had changed. His wife for twenty-two years, she now seemed to have more warmth toward the newspaper delivery guy than she showed toward him. Their endless bickering and fighting had worn him down. No matter how he tried to explain himself to her, she always seemed to take it the wrong way. Any conversation left him in a state of despair.

Deep down, all he wanted to do was to run away and not have to face her anymore, but with three teenage kids in the house, he didn't have that luxury. As hopeless as he felt, he had to deal with Aisha one way or the other. She'd completely shut down to him and now had told him she wanted out. He just did not know how he was going to handle his emotions.

I'm guessing that this is not your finest hour either and would not be surprised if at this point of your life, like Trevor, you were a bit of an emotional wreck. The end of your marriage, particularly when kids are involved, can stir up some powerful emotions. It's not unusual for those emotions to take over, making you feel profoundly hurt, anxious, enraged, stressed, or deeply guilty.

That's not true for everyone, but if it is for you, this chapter, which introduces the first of the *Seven Steps for Breaking the News*—learning to manage your own emotions—is intended to help. I know it's not easy. I want to turn the spotlight on you now to give you a perspective on your own emotions. In the next chapter, I will provide you with some techniques to help you feel more in control.

The final decision to separate is rarely one made equally by both partners. Even if you have been going to marriage counseling, if both of you have been threatening divorce, or if you've been separated in the past, the spouse who decides to pull the plug on the marriage is, at that moment, in the one-up position. Until that point, as bad as things might have been, both partners felt that they had options. But once one spouse has made up his or her mind to divorce, the other is stuck with the fact that options have dried up.

Although in some divorces both parties had toyed with ending the marriage, most divorce decisions are far more skewed. One person (the *leaver*) makes a unilateral decision that he or she wants out, and the other (the *leavee*), who doesn't want the marriage to end, is forced to participate against his or her will. In some extreme situations, the decision to divorce comes out of the blue! One partner believed that the marriage was a happy one— until the moment the other bolted, leaving the abandoned spouse completely shocked and traumatized.

If you are the *leaver*, like Aisha, you may have been agonizing about making this decision and dreading the process of taking the necessary steps to make it happen. At the point at which you are reading this book, however, you're likely very motivated to get all the tasks of separation over with as soon as possible so you can get out the door and move on with your life.

If this is your position, even though you're the *leaver*, it's no picnic for you. You may be riddled with guilt and deeply worried about how your decision will affect your children (and maybe also your soon-to-be former spouse). You may be tempted to minimize evidence of your children's distress so that you can prove to your spouse that what you're doing is not such a bad thing and that your children are going to be fine.

If you, like Trevor, are the *leavee*, you're in the gut-wrenching position of having to tell your children about a divorce that you really don't want. You may hope that they will be horrified and that their reaction will be so devastatingly negative that it might prove to the *leaver* what a destructive thing he or she is doing. To that end, the *leavee* may subconsciously sabotage the children's adjustment to the news to make the point, "Look what you're doing to us!"

You may truly be convinced that your child will be irrevocably damaged by your marriage's breakup or that he will sail through it with hardly a scratch. Whether you're the *leaver* or *leavee*, it's normal to be tempted to either exaggerate or minimize to your spouse evidence of the intensity of your child's reaction in order to bolster your agenda. There's no doubt that your child will pick this up. While giving in to this urge may feel justified now, in the long run it can be very damaging for your child.

Don't get in the habit of using your child's emotions to support *your* position! You need to make a clear distinction between attending to your child's genuine reaction and influencing that reaction to serve your own goals. We want to keep the kids out of the parents' conflict and, as much as possible, not use them to achieve our own agenda.

This was not the case for fourteen-year-old Suzy, who got caught in the middle of her parents' drama, each one using her brother and her to support their own opposing points of view. She writes, "My dad felt like we had all turned against him and let us know it. He had big tirades for everyone, listing our many, many faults. My mom was different in that she expected my brother and me to be super happy about everything and expressed her disappointment that we weren't happier for her." Suzy and her brother were in an impossible situation, pulled in two different directions by parents who had their own agendas and were not attuned to what their children really needed.

Keeping Your Kids Out of the Middle

Parents often don't see the harm in enlisting a child as an ally, particularly when they believe that the other parent's behavior is wrong. Often that "wrong" has to do with betrayals or disappointments between the adults, but parents often generalize the blame to include the kids. Although your spouse may be a good parent, you may be tempted to put him or her down to your child because you so profoundly disapprove of how *you* are being treated.

When you purposefully damage your child's bond with her other parent, you're harming your child. We have a right arm and a left arm, and they're both important. It may be unavoidable to amputate one because it's diseased, but we do this only in the most extreme of circumstances. Your child's identity includes both her mom and her dad—her right arm and her left arm. Even if one arm (or parent) does not have the most stellar of qualities, she needs both of you. Please permit her to love both of you.

It's very tempting, in an effort to punish a partner who's leaving, to want to define the leaving as a parent abandoning the *children*. Although you may feel it is wrong or immoral for your spouse to be leaving the marriage, unless your partner is actually planning to cut ties with the kids, please don't tell your kids that the parent is leaving "us".

Even if your kids have always been much closer to you than to your spouse, preserving and promoting some kind of connection with a departing parent who cares about the children, is the right thing for them in the long run. Kids get caught in the middle of the conflict, and a lot of damage can be done to the parent/child relationship when the *leaver* is demonized for his or her decision. It's not easy to compartmentalize the anger you feel toward your spouse so that his or her relationship with the kids can remain undisturbed, but I know that once some time has passed and the emotions have calmed down, you'll be proud of yourself that you did.

Controlling Your Urge to Lash Out

Many of the divorced parents who participated in the study that led to this book said that their greatest regret was that they were unable to control their emotions during *the divorce talk*. They behaved impulsively or were motivated by revenge.

Here are some of their responses to my question about what they regretted most in telling the kids:

- Carole: "Our daughter was eighteen, and I was so hysterical at just learning the news that I reacted emotionally, without thinking or planning out what I should do or say. I was not thinking of her as much as I should have been."
- Martin: "I wish I had taken more time to plan."
- Adrianna: "I revealed to the kids an intimacy problem my husband had that I felt might have been the cause of his departure. My kids had no business knowing about that. I guess I was just desperate to attach a reason to the total shocking experience. I would not do that again."
- Joanne: "I wish that the children did not have to be put in the middle of the divorce. I wish I could have been more in control of my emotions and not shown them all the pain I was going through."
- Simon: "I was probably being angrier than anything. I could have stowed the anger a bit more."

Don't make the same mistakes. You're probably getting a lot of advice from friends and family, much of it along the lines of urging you to protect yourself from your spouse or encouraging you to get back at him or her. But you'll feel better about yourself if you can manage to take the high road!

Listen to your inner voice of caution. If you're second-guessing yourself and worrying that you might regret a choice that you're about to make, don't do it! For example, you may be tempted to break the news to the kids on your own and sideline your spouse from having his or her voice heard, but if something is nagging inside of you because you know it's not right, listen to it.

You're stressed and your judgment is not at its best, so it's a good idea to let things percolate before you act on them. If you notice yourself rushing into something, sleep on it and see how things look in the morning. That will be hard to do, but the more you can think things through and act coolly and deliberately, the more likely that you will be able to protect your children and end up feeling better about yourself.

You can do this! That's why you're reading this book! It starts with reaching down and pulling up your ideal self—the person you are when you feel strong, confident, and centered—from deep inside of you. That person is in there; you've met that self before. You just need to re-find that vision of yourself now. Once you've done that, you'll be more likely to tolerate the other parent's presence without fear.

Therapist Nancy Privett outlined the energetic environment you need to create. I love what she has to say.

> The best introduction to the child regarding the changes divorce brings would have to be a product of strong intention on the part of both parents to create an energetic environment that keeps the children safe. However, that can immediately be undermined by one or both parents acting out. So, any non-traumatizing introduction to the child would need to be congruent with the intention of the parents to monitor their own behavior for the child's well being.

She is emphasizing the importance of having enough self-discipline to be able to keep your emotions in check. But you may need some help getting there and the next chapter will provide some techniques you can use to access the frame of mind you will be able to feel proud of later on.

TAKEAWAY from *Understanding Your Own Emotions*

- The different roles of *leaver* and *leavee* may cause you to either exaggerate or minimize your assessment of how the revelation is affecting your child.
- When you purposefully damage your child's relationship with the other parent, you are hurting the child most of all.
- Avoid acting impulsively or trying to exact revenge against your spouse. More than likely, you will regret such behavior in the future.
- Tune in to your most mature, non-dramatic self so that you can tell the kids in a way that does the least damage.

CHAPTER 3

Techniques for Managing Your Emotions

Many parents on the verge of talking to the kids about an upcoming divorce are in emotional turmoil and struggling to maintain their equilibrium. In this chapter, we will continue with the first of the *Seven Steps for Breaking the News*—managing your own emotions—and give you some simple techniques can help. Although you may not "click" with all the following suggestions, perhaps one or two will be useful in helping you achieve a more relaxed state of mind.

Make a Mantra to Stay Centered

One of the best ways to get in touch with your ideal emotional state when you have to deal with your spouse is to make a mantra and repeat it to yourself as needed. It centers your thinking, making it easier for you to stay focused on your positive energy, even in stressful times. You choose three words (your mantra) that describe what you'd hope to be feeling and silently repeat those words to yourself when you're facing a difficult situation.

Here's how it works. Think about what emotional state you want to be in when you meet with your spouse to discuss how to tell the kids. For example, you might want to feel calm, confident, centered, focused, neutral, parental, unemotional, determined, Zen-like, or strong. You get the idea. Let's say you've chosen "calm, focused and determined". Just before the meeting, repeat your mantra to yourself several times: *Calm, focused, determined. Calm, focused, determined. Calm, focused determined. Calm, focused, determined.*

You'll be surprised! Words have such power that just by repeating your mantra, you'll find it much easier to get into and maintain your ideal frame of mind. Your brain can't think two things at the same time. You can't be thinking, "Oh my God, I'm freaking out, I hate this, I'm so shaky!" and "Calm, focused, determined!" The words you purposefully repeat to yourself in your mantra will trump the more negative ones you'd be thinking without it.

The mantra also helps you remember who you are and what's important to you. It gives you the strength to be your best self. Stop for a moment and create your mantra. Define three qualities that make you feel good about yourself. What are they? When you have them, write them down and stick them on your computer or inside your closet door so you'll remember to use them when you need them. Feel free to change them as new situations arise.

Pour Some Steel In It to Remain Strong

Sometimes I suggest to people who are really struggling emotionally to pour some steel in their spine. Imagine that you're literally strengthening your spine with some molten steel! Sit up straight! Toughen up!

You've got a job to do—telling the kids—and you want to do it the best way possible. If you were a corporate CEO leading an important meeting, what image would you want to project? You'd definitely want to leave the wimpy, whiney you at home and show up projecting your authoritative best.

When you're actually talking with your kids about the changes that are going to be taking place in their lives, you want to present your best parental self—attuned, caring, and empathetic. That doesn't mean that you can't be sad or cry, but it does mean that you will not burden your child with the disturbing spectacle of a wailing parent whose runny nose is going unwiped! As twelve-year-old Lexi recommended to her distraught mother: "Get a therapist that *isn't* your unlicensed child!"

You can break down and let it out with your sister or brother, your parents, therapist, or friend. With your kids, however, you still need to be a parent and to pour some steel in it! Jill Jones-Soderman and Allison Quattrocchi, authors of *How to Talk to Your Children about Divorce*, wrote, "No matter how miserable you feel, do not be pitiful, dependent, self-righteous, or blaming. Your children cannot handle that on top of their own grief, nor should they ever have to."

Ground Yourself to Be Calm

You can physically ground yourself if you're feeling over-whelmed, either in a meeting with your spouse or during the ac-tual *divorce talk* itself. If you're in a highly emotional state, you can dial it down by using the following techniques to reconnect with your physical self:

- Think about your feet on the floor and imagine them planted on the earth beneath you. This will help you draw some strength from Mother Nature.
- Briefly rub the tops of your thighs with your hands and feel the heat you generate. This will help you connect with yourself.
- Mentally scan your body and identify what you're feeling physically. Notice where you're holding your tension and make a conscious effort to relax those muscles.
- Breathe! Breathe! Breathe! In through your nose, out through your mouth, slowly and consciously, turning your attention to your healing breath. This is guaranteed to help you feel more relaxed and in control.

- Notice three features in the room. Connect with your surroundings by taking note of the light coming in the window, the picture on the wall, the rug on the floor, or anything else that catches your eye. Becoming awake to your environment will help you de-stress.

Recognize That What's Extraordinary Becomes Ordinary

Another technique for managing your emotional state is to remember one of my favorite sayings, "What's extraordinary becomes ordinary." You may be in the midst of great turmoil right now, but I promise you that it's not always going to be this bad. To successfully get through the hardest things, you need to have a long term view. Once you've crossed the bridge into your new life, and after some time has passed, you will click into a *new normal* and your life will go on.

Maintaining a long term view is also important when telling the kids because their reaction to the news may be dramatic. They may, for example, say something like, "I'll never be happy again!" or "My life is ruined!" and you'll need to be able to see past this moment and know that those feelings won't last forever.

Such sentiments will soften over time as the child adjusts to the new reality. And it's the same with you. You may feel that you can never be happy again or that your life is ruined, but that's simply not true. Believe it or not, this too shall pass. You *can* refashion a happy life post-divorce!

Turn Your Spouse from Tiger to Pussycat (Psychologically Speaking)

Let me share with you a visualization exercise that will help you minimize the negative reaction you may be having whenever you have to deal with your spouse. In your mind, you may have elevated your spouse psychically to represent a dangerous opponent who has the power to hurt you. In reality, however, it's just ole George or Lindy.

Using the following visualization, you can resize your spouse in your mind so that you feel less vulnerable.

- Close your eyes and imagine your spouse as a scary animal. What animal do you visualize him or her to be?
- What are the characteristics of this animal?
- What do you fear this animal could do to you?
- With your eyes closed, expand this visualization until you can imagine this animal in all its power . . .
- Now, take a deep breath, switch gears, and transform this animal into a different, more benign form, like a cartoon character or a stuffed animal (e.g., Winnie the Pooh or the Cowardly Lion).
- What are the characteristics of this transformed animal (e.g., fuzzy ears, a floppy tail)?
- Now visualize your spouse as this declawed and defanged fluffy or animated animal.

The next time you anticipate an uncomfortable interaction, remember to transform your spouse from the threatening predator into the harmless avatar you have created.

Take the High Road to Minimize Conflict

Corinna, an elementary school teacher, had a sudden realization one day that the shock of her divorce had caused her to lose touch with her own values. She realized that she was not dealing with her children properly and had lowered her standards for her behavior. Her call to action sums up her promise to herself to remain the quality person she'd always tried to be:

> Basically, we need to rise above. My life has become a mess and I have become messy. I have noticed that a lot of profanity and outrage has entered my vocabulary. I need to become more disciplined, especially with my children. I need to behave more "professionally" with

them. If I were working with a child in my classroom, there would be certain boundaries, certain things I would not say. I think my kids have seen and heard a bit too much, and I need to protect them. I was completely destabilized by everything that happened, but I don't want that to be an excuse for poor behavior and lousy parenting.

Corinna got a grip on her emotions and was able to recognize how the turmoil of the moment permitted her to disregard what she truly held dear—behaving as a civilized adult and protecting her kids, no matter what. She woke up to how she needed to take the high road, and that's exactly what you need to do too. I know it's hard to turn the volume down in your mind on those thoughts that want to punish or hurt your spouse, particularly if you're the *leavee*. I also know you can do it!

TAKEAWAY from *Techniques for Managing Your Emotions*

- Make a mantra to stay centered and repeat it to yourself when you are facing a stressful encounter with your spouse.
- Imagine pouring some steel in your spine to help you stay strong.
- Ground yourself through the use of your mind and breath to relax your body.
- Remember that what's extraordinary becomes ordinary and that the intensity of this time in your life will settle down.
- Take the high road and don't permit yourself to lower the standards by which you behave.

CHAPTER 4

The Planning Meeting

When Wes told Wendy that he was leaving her, the bottom fell out of her world. Married for nine years, theirs had seemed to be a happy union. He was the love of her life, and she'd always believed that he was every bit as happy as she was. He'd been a great father, obviously besotted with three-year-old Maya. For the past year or so, they had been trying to get pregnant again, but so far, no luck. Wendy knew he'd been irritable recently but thought that was because his new supervisor at work seemed intent on making his life miserable.

When Wes revealed that he was moving right in with his girlfriend, Wendy couldn't believe it. It was surreal, but it *was* happening. It was out of her control. She made Wes promise one thing—that he wouldn't tell anyone, not his sister, their friends, their parents, anyone, until she was ready. Out of guilt, he agreed.

Wendy was an emotional wreck, but within a week Wes turned on the pressure, insisting that he could only stick with the vow of silence for so long. He was ready to move out and, after ten days of misery, he couldn't wait any longer. Seeing Mommy crying, Maya had been asking over and over what was wrong, but all Wendy would say was that something had happened in her family that was making her very sad.

For Wendy, the *leavee*, absorbing the reality of an unexpected, unwanted divorce is an arduous internal process that will take a long time to work through—minimally a year and more likely two. For the *leavee*, the tsunami hits without warning, and there is an overwhelming amount to process. Meanwhile, the *leaver*, like Wes, has the luxury of choosing the ideal timing for him. He's digested the implications and is ready.

Ready or not, the act of telling the children that their parents are separating makes the fact of divorce real. Before taking that step, there's always the fantasy that you can turn back. But most parents feel that once they've told the kids, it's a fait accompli—it's going to happen.

Content of The Planning Meeting

In a perfect world, you would have an effective planning meeting with your spouse before you tell the kids so that you can get your stories straight. Unfortunately, in many situations a nice, refined sit-down is out of the question. If you know that things are too volatile and that working together to plan what to tell the kids will inevitably do more damage than good, skip it. This would be the case, for example, if one or both of you are unable to control your emotions and are using any opportunity to either attack or cajole.

You could benefit from engaging the help of an appropriate third party who cares about you both and is known to be balanced and not inflammatory. If you don't have a handy friend or family member who fits the bill, it's worth meeting with a trained family therapist or divorce mediator even for one session of planning.

In this chapter, we'll address the second of the *Seven Steps for Breaking the News*—have a planning meeting. If there is any way you two can manage to have a productive planning meeting conversation however, go for it. The breakdown of a marriage is inherently a chaotic time, and anything that serves to create some order and structure helps. The planning meeting should not be an ambitious affair. If you can agree on who is going to tell the kids, and when and where, you're way ahead of the game. The statements you come up with to explain why you're separating don't have to be brilliant. Something like,

"Your mom and I have decided that we're not going to be living together anymore" is already a ton of information for any child to absorb. Keep it simple!

Sometimes people are afraid of the planning meeting because by the time they're at that point, the interests of the "we" have morphed into protecting just the "me." They no longer trust their spouse. You may have become adversaries and worry that anything you say can and will be held against you in a court of law. So remember that the planning meeting is not intended to draw up a preliminary separation agreement. All you are going to do is clarify some of the details of *the divorce talk* and co-create a story that your child can understand of why Mommy and Daddy are not going to be living together anymore. No more. No less. You just need to let them know that the family will be changing and give them something to hold on to by way of an explanation. Let them know the specifics of what will be happening next—who will live where, for example—if you have this information

There will be plenty of opportunities later, when reality starts to sink in, to explain more to the kids, if it's appropriate. In later chapters, we'll go into detail about what to say and what not to say. For now, I just want to emphasize the value of holding a planning meeting as a way of organizing the important information you need to relay to your child. You probably don't see eye-to-eye about what to say and how to break this news, but to whatever extent you can come to a consensus, your kids will benefit.

Define it as "a planning meeting about what to tell the kids" and make sure that that is the only topic discussed. If the conversation digresses onto any other topic, gently but firmly bring it back by saying, "Let's focus on what to tell the kids." Don't either initiate or allow yourself to be drawn off course into an agonizing discussion of the breakdown of the marriage. That doesn't advance your goal of hammering out an agreement on a few key points.

Here is the agenda for what Wendy and Wes (and you and your spouse) need to discuss in the planning meeting. Each parent should do some thinking about these points prior to getting together to talk about them. (Upcoming chapters will make in-depth recommendations about how to handle everything else on this list.)

- Who is going to break the news to Maya that her parents are getting separated?
- Where and when will they tell her?
- What reason will they give for the separation?
- When is the separation going to take place?
- What plans do they have for her living arrangements after the separation?
- What can they do to make sure they are truly attuned to Maya's feelings after she has been told, and to give her as much space as she needs to express whatever she might be feeling?

Write down what you have come up with and both keep a copy. Following the meeting, take some time to think about what you have agreed upon and then come back for a wrap-up session later to make sure you are still both on the same page.

Maya doesn't need to know that Dad has someone else in his life at this point. Give her as much time as possible to adjust to the big changes taking place before you introduce another earth-shaking piece of information. Of course she will need to be informed because he's moving in with the affair partner, but just not during the first *divorce talk*.

Remaining on Track Toward a Productive Meeting

You are trying to get something accomplished here so you have to be on your best behavior, starting with the following two essential rules for the planning meeting:

- Keep your ego out of it. You have to learn how to talk about your child in a safe, protected way, or else you'll never get anywhere!

- No surprises. Don't use the planning meeting to spring something disturbing on your spouse. That's counter-productive.

Consider handling this session as a proper business meeting. You're trying to get something accomplished. Remember that! As Elizabeth S. Thayer and Jeffrey Zimmerman wrote in *The Co-Parenting Survival Guide,* "Don't try to win, try to solve." Here are eight points that should *not* be on your agenda: attacking, blaming, punishing, pleading, sarcasm, provocation, going over marital issues, and trying to make the other feel guilty.

Therapist Nancy Privett describes the frame of mind you need to be in when you are planning for *the divorce talk* this way: "I can imagine that there are ways to tell a child about divorce without traumatization, but it would mean that both parents were stable, grounded, invested, compassionate and willing to co-create on behalf of the kids and have the children's best interests first and foremost."

Stable, grounded, invested, compassionate, and willing to co-create! Both of you! So that's the goal to keep in mind as you work your way through this process. More than likely you won't be able to accomplish it all the time, but it's the road map of where to go.

You want to use the planning meeting as a chance to step away from the marital struggle that you've been going through and embark on the new relationship as co-parents. To keep the focus on the kids, it's a good idea to have a photo of them on the table in front of you and to remember to talk to each other in such a way that you wouldn't be ashamed if they could hear you—but, of course, make sure they are well out of earshot!

A Truce to Help the Process Along

You may even propose a truce, if there is conflict in your relationship right now. The truce will be in effect when you are talking about what to tell the kids and, definitely, while you are doing the actual *divorce talk*. The concept of a truce is useful. It defines the need for a cease-fire for a specific period of time and is an idea that you can wrap your mind around.

Here's an excerpt from Thayer and Zimmerman's *The Co-Parenting Survival Guide* that outlines how to have a constructive conversation when the stress level is high:

- Take your time—Angry responses are often impulsive.
- Listen, Listen, Listen—High conflict people like to talk but don't really listen.
- Can I finish PLEASE! —High conflict parents don't let each other finish a thought.
- Let's talk nicely—High conflict parents often lack rules. They feel that they can say just about anything they want in any way they want.
- The past is the past—It's not helpful to rehash old issues.
- Keep it short and simple—Communications that are too lengthy are often not heard.
- Relax—Stress management techniques work.
- Focus on your communication goals—Be clear about the message you want to communicate.
- Seek to understand.
- Pay attention to your non-verbal communication.

The planning meeting must most definitely *not* be a long, drawn-out, painful ordeal. If you've both given it some thought and you enter into it determined to keep the focus on making progress, you can achieve something in twenty minutes or a half hour.

Avoiding Doing Damage

If you run into a roadblock that threatens to make the process deteriorate, in the interest of not doing any more damage, it's best to back off and come back later—but only if it's possible to accomplish something. Rule of thumb: when things get gruesome, stop the conversation and cool off. Here are a few clues that tell you that it's time to end the exercise:

- Someone is consistently trying to outtalk the other.
- Tables are being slammed, shoes are being thrown, feet are being stamped.
- One of you is swearing: the s-word, f-word, b-word—any of those alphabet words that you don't like your kids to use.
- Your anger or frustration level crosses 7 on a scale of 1 to 10.
- Your body is getting into a high state of arousal: blood pressure rising, you hear ringing in your ears, your hands are getting sweaty.

Uh-oh! That conversation is going nowhere, so give it up and consider engaging that third party to help. Don't feel you failed – a successful planning meeting is hard to accomplish when there is tension in your relationship. Think of it as a temporary detour. At least you tried to make the planning meeting work.

TAKEAWAY from *The Planning Meeting*

- Using your new skills to stay centered, conduct this meeting as if it's literally a business meeting. You want to walk away with a concrete plan that is doable!
- Define what you want to accomplish.
- Don't try to discuss too much. A few well-defined points are far more valuable than a long, complex document that reads like a separation agreement.
- Keep the focus on the plans for your child, and don't use the discussion as an excuse to attack or entreat your spouse. You don't have the luxury of being emotionally sloppy when you're trying to get something done.
- Summarize what you've agreed upon in written form and both keep a copy.

CHAPTER 5

What Divorce Means to Kids

Not all children are distressed when they learn that their parents are separating. For some, it's welcome news. Rebecca, who was four years old at the time of her parents' divorce, remembers:

> My sister was upset about the divorce, so she was crying while my mom held her. I was dancing a little jig, not understanding what all of the crying was about. To my four-year-old mind there was no reason for tears. In fact, I felt almost happy and relieved. I knew my dad wasn't safe or helpful or an appropriate part of our family. I danced a little jig and tried to jolly them out of their strange (to me) emotional response. The only weird part was that the crying of my mom and my sister made me wonder why I didn't feel the same way. I felt removed from their pain, had no access to it because I genuinely felt pleased that someone was making a wise plan for the future. I could not understand why anyone would cry about that.

Rebecca's reaction definitely goes counter to what we'd expect from a little girl whose daddy was standing on the threshold with his bags packed but due to the level of tension in her family, it made sense and was a good turn of events.

Why is learning that their parents are getting divorced such a devastating event in the lives of some kids and even possibly good news for others? What aspects of *the divorce talk* have the potential to do the most damage? What are the real transitional events embedded in this telling? What are the hidden psychological disturbances? This chapter helps you accomplish the third of the *Seven Steps for Breaking the News*—understanding the meaning of the divorce for your particular kids.

When asked about their first reaction to hearing the news that their parents were getting divorced, many participants in the study said they felt one of two diametrically opposed emotions. A small number were, like Rebecca, relieved. These were the kids from families in which the fighting was intolerable, and they were just glad to hear that it was going to be over soon. Some of them had thought that their parents' relationship was just wrong, and they knew it would be better for everyone for them to separate.

Other kids describe their emotions on hearing about the divorce in less pragmatic terms. Here are some of their thoughts:

- Christine, 13 at the time, felt "Like there was a hole in me. Afraid. Not sure what would happen next."
- Trevor, 5, was "Hateful, enraged, bitter."
- Sixteen-year-old Jamie describes feeling "Unexpectedly shocked, considering the thought never really left my mind that they didn't belong together."
- Hilary, at 15, felt "Devastated. Angry. Sad. Resentment. Hurt."
- Twenty-year-old Genevieve was "Destroyed. Crying, I fell to my knees, couldn't walk, had to crawl!"

What's happening in the minds of these kids to cause these painful primitive emotions? If we were to frankly analyze what actually occurs when we inform kids of an impending divorce, drained of the emotional meaning, we would see that what we are actually doing is simply announcing some changes. Here are the headlines:

- Your parents will no longer be a married couple.

- They will no longer be living together in the same place.

Further, these two fundamental changes lead to other tangible changes, such as:

- You won't see both parents every day.
- You might not continue living in the same house or going to the same school.
- The family will have a new definition, as a divorced family.

If we look at these facts in black and white, they don't seem so earthshaking. For example, it's not unusual for a family to move to a new home or for kids to change schools, and if a parent travels a lot for work or does shift work, the kids may well not see him or her every day. So clearly, it's not the concrete fact of where they live and how often they see their parent that leads to such emotional pain.

So, it's the meaning of divorce that leads kids to experience the wrenching sadness. If we were to reboot the scene and install full-spectrum color and emotion, we begin to see aspects beyond the geographical changes that divorce brings. Those aspects that trigger the intense emotional response may include:

- Witnessing the emotional pain of one or both parents
- Being aware of tense or angry interchanges between the parents
- Feeling sad about the prospect of missing a parent
- Worrying about one or both parents or about siblings
- Feeling insecure about unknown changes to come regarding concrete things, like living arrangements
- Worrying about unknown changes to everything else, as well.

Deeper Meaning of Divorce to Kids

There is, however, an even deeper level of meaning for kids that is at the core of their distress. Many children feel at least one, or even several, of the following emotions:

- *Anger* at not having any control over important events in their lives
- *Guilt* if they believe that the family split is the result of something they did
- *Shame* at being in a divorced family, which feels like a failure
- *Insecurity*, because life has become unpredictable
- *Anxiety* as a result of seeing a level of despair in a parent
- *Fear*, because a parent has become unrecognizable in his or her current disorganized state of mind
- *Abandoned*, because the distraught parents are unavailable to provide the usual level of care and support
- *Burdened*, because it falls on their shoulders to support their parents or siblings
- *Betrayed* that their parents, entrusted to make life safe, have subjected them to risk
- *Loss of respect* for their parents, who are behaving in ways that seem dramatic, childish, or hypocritical
- *Confused*, because they don't really understand what's going on
- *Shocked*, because they never thought this could happen to them
- *Traumatized*, because they feel all alone in a life that has changed

The list is daunting, I know, but it describes fairly comprehensively how some children experience the revelation of their parents' divorce. That's good, because with this knowledge you can put into place as many safeguards as possible to address these

underlying issues and help your child maintain his equilibrium—
or regain it as quickly as possible.

We will talk about how you can avoid most of the pitfalls that
lead to children experiencing the emotions listed above. Although
we can't eliminate the risk of your child feeling deeply sad, we
can control whether he feels fearful, burdened, confused, abandoned, guilty, anxious, and all alone.

The revelation of divorce is so hard because, typically, it is
not consistent with the child's understanding of his life and who
his parents are. Children want to idealize their parents and don't
have the experience to understand that parents can be vulnerable,
needy, lonely, sexually dissatisfied, hungry for love, disconnected,
bored, narcissistic, and all the other elements that may contribute
to the breakup of a marriage.

Many children can't wrap their mind around the fact that one
parent's needs can take precedence over the needs of the other
parent or of the family. So in hearing about the divorce, they
struggle to understand how their parents could be so different
from the people they thought they knew.

Powerlessness

Psychologist Joan B. Kelly and lawyer Mary Kay Kisthardt wrote:
"Separation is the ending of the family as they have known it and
children have no vision of what will follow or what will happen
to them. Even when marriages or partnerships had significant
and evident conflict or difficulties, most children seemed to have
little emotional preparation for the parental decision to separate
and divorce and they reacted to hearing about the separation and
divorce with shock, disbelief, distress, anxiety, and anger."

In my work with children from divorced families, I've often
heard kids express one predominant emotion, and that's powerlessness. Kids whose parents get divorced often are incredulous
that no one ever asked *them* what *they* wanted. They're outraged
that such an important decision that affects them so fundamen-

tally could take place without their consent. Eight-year-old Nicolas told me that if his parents really loved him, they would listen to what *he* wanted and NOT GET DIVORCED!

This theme is particularly prevalent in our twenty-first century child-centered society in which kids are consulted about everything! Five year olds are asked which restaurant they want to go to, twelve year olds pick their high schools, and fifteen year olds participate in choosing the family car. For many children, hearing that their parents are getting divorced may be the first time that a major family decision has been made without their having a say in the matter.

Some kids feel outraged by this turn of events and let you know it as vocally as possible. If yours is a highly child-centered family and your kids expect to be consulted about family decisions, don't be surprised if they fight this change in their status. It will take them some time to adjust to the fact that this is one family decision in which they cannot participate.

TAKEAWAY from *What Divorce Means to Kids*

- Inherent in the separation are the potential of several levels of meaning for your child.
- Once you are aware of the possible hidden meanings and powerful emotions that may arise, you will learn how to help your child with them.
- This may be the first time your child has not been consulted about a big decision being made in the family, which may lead to a feeling of powerlessness.

CHAPTER 6

Will Your Child See it Coming?

In this chapter, we will continue exploring the third of the *Seven Steps for Breaking the News*—understanding the meaning of the divorce for your particular kids. There is another important aspect of kids' experience that has a profound effect on how they will react to the news, and that's the extent to which the news comes as a surprise. Every divorcing family is different, and prior to the moment of separation parents have revealed their level of marital unhappiness to their kids in a continuum of intensity.

Vibe at Home—The Openly High-Conflict Household

At one end of the spectrum are the couples who are screaming and yelling on a regular basis. There is high drama: one parent or the other storming out, sleeping on the couch, going back to their parents' home overnight, cursing, separating and reuniting, going for counseling, and threatening divorce. Often the kids are right in the middle of the mayhem, taking sides, pleading for calm, or shaking silently in their beds at night, trying to plug their ears to the noise below. These are the families in which, as for four-year-old Rebecca, word of the divorce may be welcome news and the primary reaction of the child may be relief.

You would think that kids in these families would not be surprised when news of the divorce is finally announced, but remarkably, that's not always the case.

- Amanda, who was 10 at the time of her parents' divorce, said, "Although there were many fights, some extremely destructive, and my father did leave sometimes, I never expected the marriage to end, because even though things are bad or not the norm, you never want your family to break up, because that's the life you know."
- Donna, also 10, remembered, "Even though my parents had separated multiple times, my sister and I were shocked and devastated."
- Sixteen-year-old Nick wrote, "I can't say that their marriage ending was truly a bad thing, or all that surprising. If anything it was remarkable that they made it to almost twenty years. My parents' arguments were a persistent element of my childhood. They rarely seemed to be on the same page about anything and there were often suspicions of infidelity."

If your child definitely knows that things are bad, it helps if he can talk about it. You can open a discussion with your son by saying, "I guess you know that Mom and I have been fighting a lot recently" or "You've probably felt the tension in the house between Daddy and me." This may already be a big statement for your child, particularly if you've not openly addressed the high-conflict environment in the household with him. If your child has seen a lot, even if nothing has been said, he definitely has had a reaction to all of that. This is your chance to listen, with attunement, to what life has been like in the midst of a parental whirlwind.

Invite him to tell you what he's been experiencing, recognizing that what you hear may not be pretty. Your job is to have big ears and a small mouth. Your role is to listen and not pounce on whatever is being said to use as ammunition against your spouse à la, "See what you're putting him through!?" In an upcoming chapter, I'll give you the tools you need to be able to help your child unburden himself and finally say the truth of what he is feeling.

Vibe at Home — The Well-Contained High-Conflict Household

Rather than having open, angry fights, yours may be the kind of home in which there are serious issues but the conflict isn't really all that verbally expressed. Perhaps you've been able to keep your problems very separate from your kids, so they have been relatively unaware of the severity of the discord. They may have seen you fight occasionally, but it hasn't been an everyday occurrence.

You may be conflict avoiders and the type of couple who rarely or never fights (overtly). The tension between you exists, but it's under the radar as far as your kids are concerned. The kids are not too concerned about the coldness between you or the fact that you never seem to do things together, because they are getting plenty of your attention for themselves. You may have focused on being good parents and avoided dealing with whatever was not working in the marriage, so the children are relatively clueless.

- This was the case in the household of 12-year-old Bruce: "Everything in the household was quiet. My parents didn't communicate at all, which was the eventual downfall of their marriage. The only thing out of the ordinary was that my parents always, always slept in different spaces—my father in the bed, my mother on the couch. I had never, ever known them to sleep in the same bed."
- Letty, 12, wrote: "I wasn't expecting it would come to an end, and it did come to a surprise. From one day to the next, I was a child in a broken home. Aside from the usual arguments of finances, I wouldn't say they fought a lot. There was no tension between them."

Vibe at Home—The No-Conflict Household

At the other end of the spectrum from the yellers and screamers are the couples I wrote about in my book, *Runaway Husbands,* which explores the phenomenon of Wife Abandonment Syndrome—when a man leaves out of the blue from what his wife believed to have been a happy marriage. Although my book was about marriages in which husbands suddenly leave, wives also sometimes end their marriages without warning their spouse.

These marriages tend to end quickly and dramatically, with the majority of *leavers* moving out of the house the same day or within a couple of days of telling the unsuspecting *leavee* that it's over. Sometimes the departing spouse doesn't inform the other until *after* he or she has moved out. There is almost always an affair partner on the scene.

As a result, the abandoned spouse is devastated and typically unable to attend very effectively to the needs of the kids because she's so traumatized herself. Because of the high level of intense emotion, which has not had time to settle down, it's often very hard for the parents to sit down together to talk to the children. Out of the blue separations are most likely to lead to a painful scene when the kids are informed, and it is here that parents are challenged to rise to their best self in order to protect their children from being caught in the middle.

The kids in these families are as shocked as the abandoned spouse, because the other parent's departure came as a surprise to them, too. These kids are at high risk of experiencing trauma when they learn about the divorce. Later we will focus on this very essential issue—how to minimize the risk of *the divorce talk* becoming a traumatic event in the child's life.

So within this continuum, from the plate throwers to the frozen smilers to the runaways, there are all sorts of other couple relationships; ones characterized by criticism, snide sarcasm, and subtle put-downs to those defined by stony silence, conflict avoidance, and everything in between.

Defining Your Child's Situation

Let's take a look at the possible position your child has been in with regard to the problems in your marriage. Which boxes would you check?

❑ He believes our relationship to be happy, stable, and secure.
❑ He's relatively oblivious to the nature of our troubled relationship.
❑ The kids see us bicker and fight but assume that it's just normal.
❑ She's felt responsible, from time to time, to try to improve things or intervene in our relationship, even if we have not encouraged her to do so.
❑ She's very aware of the tensions in our relationship and is encouraged by one or both of us to either take sides or try to calm things down.
❑ He feels closely connected to one of us, although he is not hostile to the other.
❑ He is strongly allied with and protective of one of us and blames the other for the problems.

Obviously, it is very important to be aware of the role your child has played in the marriage relationship, because it will greatly influence how she will react when informed about the impending separation. Although you can't undo the past, now that you understand the role your child has played, you can start to work to soften the fallout.

The Prep-Talk

In situations where kids have no idea that there are problems between the parents, it's a good idea to prepare them with a prep-talk. The purpose is to let them know that you've been having some problems or are seeing a marriage counselor. Nobody likes to be taken by surprise. The prep-talk, which can take place a week or so before the actual *divorce talk*, starts to prepare them for the possibility that things may change and opens their minds to some extent.

Psychologist Robert E. Emery writes that it's important to give kids some warning that there's trouble brewing. He says that children who have no inkling that there is a problem can be: "stunned, greatly distressed, and sometimes even feel betrayed when they discover that life with two of the people they may feel they know better than anyone in the world was not what they believed. Scientists have found that when conflict is low in the two-parent family, children have more problems following a separation than they did when their parents were together. A degree of awareness of their parents' problems acts something like an inoculation."

The prep-talk can be a relatively casual statement over dinner like, "I thought you guys should know that Daddy and I have been having some problems and have been seeing a marriage counselor" or "I went over to spend the afternoon at Auntie Lucy's because your mom and I had a fight."

What you're doing is introducing a new thought. If the kids ask at this point, "What's happening? Are you getting a divorce?" you can answer with, "We don't really know. We're not sure what direction we're going in."

Change

This event in your child's life and in your life is all about change. Our tendency is to not want things to change. Change is scary. We can't envision what is coming next. But there is no way in life to avoid it. Life is always shifting and changing. Help your child recognize that change is unsettling at first because you can't picture what comes next, but that people usually do adjust to changes and that there is sometimes even some good as well as bad in changes we don't want. What's extraordinary becomes ordinary.

It's a huge life lesson—not to fear change but to keep an open mind to it and make a personal promise that eventually, some- how, you will turn the change to your advantage and grow from it. I suppose now I'm talking to you, as well as suggesting what you can say to your child. If you can absorb that lesson and pass it on to your kids, they will be more prepared for whatever life has in store.

TAKEAWAY from *Will Your Child See it Coming?*

- Define how evident the level of conflict has been in your household because it will affect how your child will react.
- If your child is completely unprepared for the news, you should use a prep-talk to prepare him before the actual *divorce talk*.
- Your approach to telling your kids provides a lesson for them in how to handle change in life.

CHAPTER 7

Who Should Tell

The desperation in Anne-Marie's voice was palpable when she called to make an appointment to discuss how to tell the kids. Things in her relationship were unraveling quickly and it looked like Kitty, her partner of fifteen years, was planning to move out soon. The pressure, however, was that the twins, eleven-year-old Charlie and Courtney, were leaving for camp in just five days. Should they tell them what was happening before camp and risk ruining their summer, or should they fake it till they returned in August? Anne-Marie pleaded for the soonest appointment possible. What were they going to do?

When parents come to my office to discuss how to tell the kids, often the first thing on their minds are questions about specifics, such as when is the best time, should they tell all the kids at the same time, who should do the telling, where should they hold this discussion? Of course they want to know what to tell, but the concrete details are less contentious and more manageable so are often raised first. In the next chapter, we will explore when and where to tell. But first, let's start with who should tell the kids. There are three approaches parents can take to break the news: synchronized, tandem, and solo.

Who Should Tell? — Synchronized Telling

Synchronized telling means that both parents sit down with the children and tell them together in a manner that seems relatively civil. It's best for parents to be equally involved in explaining things to the children, but even if just one parent is doing the actual telling, when they are both present, they're signally to the children that they remain an integrated parental unit.

Psychologists Nicholas Long and Rex Forehand suggest in their book, *Making Divorce Easier on Your Child*, that telling the children together demonstrates that both parents are committed to being involved in the parenting in the future. Participants in my study unanimously endorsed having both parents tell their children together. They also made it clear that it was very important to them that their parents behaved in a manner that was calm and respectful. Here's some advice from study kids who lived it:

- Bridget, 12, said, "Make sure both parents are in the room, and as much as possible, they should agree on what will be said. The parents should be kind to one another during this discussion."
- Ryan, 11, wrote, "Try to tell the story together when you are both calm. Think about the good of everyone concerned —not just how *you* come out looking. In other words, no good parent–bad parent scenarios."
- Leigh Anne, 13, said, "It's not just how you tell them, it's being able to become friends and be civil with each other. You're still a team. Team 'Mom-and-Dad!' Don't do any messy shit in front of the kids."
- Whitney, 7, related, "As hard as it was for me, the fact that they did it together was good. I knew that they both loved me and cared about me, or they would not have both been there. They let me know that whatever differences they had between them, when it came to me they could both be there for me."

Psychologist M. Gary Neuman explores a child's experience as she witnesses the emotional pain of one of the parents. He wrote:

> Often only one parent really wants the separation, and so the other may remain silent through the meeting or even seem withdrawn, tearful, and possibly fearful. You can be sure that your children will be paying more attention to the silent parent than the one who is speaking. To children, a silent, withdrawn presence telegraphs powerlessness, resignation, lack of control, and hurt. Most children would interpret this parent's demeanor to mean that he or she is being hurt by the parent who wants the divorce. If you are that saddened parent, be aware of how your expression of that attitude will only hurt your child.

Sometimes one parent takes control and the other parent listens, but the parent who does the talking doesn't present the information in a respectful, neutral way. Instead, the speaker blames or criticizes the other parent, either overtly or by using *strategic ambiguity*—saying negative things about the other parent without out-and-out putting him or her down. A parent doesn't even need to say a word to send a negative message—a smirk speaks volumes! Most children know their parents well enough to easily read the code and pick up what's going on, and they hate that. If they feel protective of the parent being criticized, it will upset them. Even if not, they may feel badly about the guilty pleasure of seeing a parent belittled.

I've often heard of the *leavee* punishing the *leaver* by insisting that he or she do the telling. Although this tactic may feel good to the rejected spouse at the moment, the child is almost sure to sense that the parent is using *the divorce talk* for some ulterior motive. That's not the best thing for the child. This happened to Bridget, who was twelve when her father told her that her parents were splitting: "My mother told me that she forced my father to tell me alone so he'd have to suffer the consequences, which, in reality, didn't punish him but me, because it set me up to take sides. Because my mother wasn't in the room during the discussion, it was implicit, even to a twelve year old, that she did not agree with the decision."

The child should be told by the parent who can be the most straightforward, sensitive, and honest—the one who will be able to do the telling in the best way possible. Researcher Joan B. Kelly suggests that the parent who has traditionally provided the most responsible and protective care for the children should take responsibility for talking to them.

Who Should Tell? — Telling in Tandem

Although many therapists recommend that both parents always tell children together, I don't agree that this is universally the best approach. If the level of tension between the parents is unbearably high and there is a risk that *the divorce talk* may deteriorate into sarcasm, sobbing, blaming, or God forbid, a screaming fight, it's better to cushion the kids from this distressing scene by telling them in tandem.

Telling kids in tandem means that one parent talks alone with the child, and then the other one does. Although the explanations given by the parents may not be in sync, at least this approach protects the child from having to be put through the painful spectacle of sitting with parents who are angry or suffering.

Who Should Tell? — Solo Telling

The majority of study participants told me that they learned about the divorce from one parent solo, usually their mom. Those discussions were often very brief, typically lasting a few minutes or less, or pared down to a sentence or two. This was the case for ten-year-old Trudy, who learned her parents were separating this way: "My dad just left, and Mom just said, 'He's gone' and cried."

Sometimes the mom or dad tells the kids solo *without* consulting the other parent, in order to put his or her own spin on the message and control how the children will understand what's going on. That impulse typically doesn't come from the noblest of places and sets a very bad precedent of manipulating the kids to serve the parent's agenda.

Solo telling, however, is necessary in certain cases, such as when one parent is unwilling or unable to participate, either because that parent is away, has abandoned the family, is suffering from mental illness, or has an addiction problem. Solo telling may also be necessary when one of the parents is so depressed and in such bad shape that it's too difficult to face the children. Sadly, that parent avoids the whole thing because he or she is not emotionally stable enough to deal with the situation.

Debbie, ten at the time, wrote: "My father was not there but now being asked this question, I realize I wish he was. It kind of feels like he didn't care about how any of his kids felt about it and just let my mother deal with it all." Having worked in therapy with men who walked away without talking to their kids, I know that many deeply regret having handled it like that—but, at the time, they just couldn't find a way to face it. They were filled with shame and felt they didn't have the skills to find the right thing to say to their kids that might help make an impossible situation better.

Whether telling the kids together or solo, you can invite another neutral, supportive person whom the child trusts (like a grandparent, uncle, or family friend who's connected to both parents) to join in *the divorce talk*. That person must be someone who has a good, stabilizing influence on the child and will not take sides.

Who Should Tell? — Telling the Kids before Telling Your Spouse

Some parents tell the child *before* informing their spouse that the marriage is over. There are various reasons that a parent might choose to do this, from the most devious of trying to lock in the child's loyalty to the understandable need to avoid a potentially volatile situation when there is fear of spousal or child abuse.

In the former case, the parent has a little respect for the spouse and is far more focused on building an alliance with the child. That preempting parent may be using the child as a support or justification for the separation when he or she finally tells the spouse that it's over—"Even Alison thinks I should leave you!"

In the latter case, a parent who is afraid of potential violence may need to get to a safe place with the kids before eliciting the anger of the abusive spouse by informing of the intention to separate. This is a legitimate reason to inform the children prior to the spouse. Safety is always primary.

TAKEAWAY from *Who Should Tell*

- Depending on what would be best for your child, choose *synchronized*, *tandem*, or *solo telling*.
- The obvious choice to lead in the telling is the parent who traditionally provided the most hands-on parenting.
- Unless there is a risk of violence, don't tell your child that the marriage is over before you tell your spouse.

CHAPTER 8

When and Where to *Tell*

In this chapter, we will continue with the fourth of the *Seven Steps for Breaking the News*. We have explored the question of who is the best person to tell the kids. Here we will look at a few more specifics primary to *the divorce talk*.

Should You Tell All the Kids at the Same Time?

There is not one universal answer to the question of whether to tell your children together in a group or one by one. You need to think through the situation in your family and make your decision based on the following:

- What is the relationship between the kids? Are your children likely to be loving and supportive of each other, or do they use any opportunity to swipe at each other and blame? In families where the siblings have a critical, competitive, or bullying relationship, you may want to tell each kid separately so that he or she can feel free to talk with you openly without worrying about being teased or put down.
- Are the children in different positions regarding how much they know about what's going on? For example, if a fifteen year old had stumbled upon an e-mail correspondence between Dad and his girlfriend and had the heartbreaking task of informing Mom about the affair, but his ten-year-old

brother knows nothing, you would want to talk with the boys separately.

- Is there a big gap between the children's ages or ability to understand? The explanation you give your toddler will be different from the one you give your teen. If there is one child who is developmentally delayed, you may need to craft a special explanation that will suit her best.
- Do your kids have very different personalities? Is one quiet and introspective and the other reactive and dramatic? You may want to talk to them separately so you can give them each your full attention and relate according to their style.
- Are you living in a blended family in which one or both of you have children from a previous marriage? This complex family structure may mean that, after the separation, the children will not continue in a parent-child relationship with the stepparent. Depending on how long the child has lived with the stepparent and the nature of that relationship, it is sometimes better for each biological parent to inform his or her kids separately.

In spite of these points, however, telling all the kids together at the same time regardless of their ages or level of understanding is best. That way, the siblings are going through it together with the only people who are in their exact boat. They can help each other, talk together, and compare notes later on. The older child can protect the younger, and the younger one can depend on the older—and that builds their relationship. Even when there is a big difference in age, you can give the simpler explanation to the group and then flesh it out later, one-on-one with an older child.

The Kids' Book of Divorce from the Fayerweather Street School suggests that all the kids be told at the same time, because then no one feels left out or like a second-class citizen. Divorce is a big secret to keep, and the kids who are told later will feel badly. Here are a couple of suggestions from moms in the study who have been through it:

- Ronit wrote: "I told my girls together with their father. One daughter sat and cried, and the other ran off. If I had it to do again, I might tell them separately, so I could deal with each reaction with full concentration."
- Sheila said: "If there is more than one child, I believe all should be told together unless there are reasons to do otherwise (i.e., ability to understand, big gaps in age, distance). A family meeting would be the best place."

When to Tell the Kids

If possible, you want to tell the kids when the initial uproar in your own life has settled down somewhat so that you can focus on breaking the news in a mature and measured way. Of course, if your wife moved out this morning and is already on the plane to Rio, you may not have that luxury. But we are always aiming for a best-case scenario, one in which you've had some time to compose yourself and prepare your message.

You will be better able to avoid saying something you might regret later if you give yourself enough time after the decision to separate has been made before you let the kids in on the news. With the goal in mind of presenting your children with a calm, well-thought-out plan, you will have to rein in your anxiety and temper your wish to get the kids on board quickly. In other words, if you possibly can, hold your horses!

Next, think through the timing with regard to important events taking place in the family. Austin, one of the participants in the study, was sixteen at the time he was told and writes: "They did it on Thanksgiving Day. My dad did most of the talking while my mom looked crushed. It was at the dining room table after we had finished eating." Really? His parents couldn't wait a day and not ruin the holiday for Austin for the rest of his life? What were they thinking?

I know you won't make that same mistake, but think about the timing from your child's point of view. Sometimes it's tricky.

If the separation is planned for the summer, as in Anne-Marie's case from the previous chapter, and the kids are going to camp, do you want to tell them before and have it hanging over their heads while they're away? Or would it be better to tell them after and risk having them feel angry that important things were going on in the family that they didn't know about?

I've worked with dozens of kids in similar situations and, by and large, they hate being out of the loop on major changes in their families. If we were to be attuned to the emotional effect of the revelation of an impending separation, I would suggest that Anne-Marie and Kitty tell the kids before they leave for camp.

There's no perfect answer, but as distressing as it is to know your parents are separating, I believe it is more distressing to return home from a month away to find your life completely changed without warning. I'm not saying that is the right answer for everyone. You know your own child and how she reacts to surprises or transitions. Put yourself in her shoes, and think long and hard about which *she* would prefer.

You will not be able to control all the variables that could affect timing. If your daughter is on the debating team and in the running for the state championship, or if your son has the lead in the school play and the whole household is busy helping him learn his lines and memorize all the songs, you will want to hang on, if you can, until those events are over before discussing separation with them. But, if you can't wait, for whatever reason, you will have to go ahead and inform them while, at the same time, trying to support those other important events in their lives as best as you can.

Parents often ask whether they need to have all the living arrangements and custody plans sewn up before telling the kids. My response is that the more *the divorce talk* takes place in an atmosphere of calm and order, the better it is for your child. So if the parent who is moving out has found a new apartment and knows when he or she will be moving, and if the decision has been made regarding how often the child will be living with each parent, the more likely it is that he will feel secure and less anxious about all the changes to come.

Imagine that you work for a company that has relocated you to another city. They tell you, "Don't worry, there is a lot of good housing available in your new city. We know you'll find a nice neighborhood and a great place to live once you get there." Yes, they're trying to reassure you, but it doesn't feel very convincing.

Now, what if they instead said, "We've found you a lovely three-bedroom townhouse in an area called Greenfield Park, which is an upscale residential district right by the lake with a lot of services for you and your kids"? You're still being relocated, but it's much more comforting to have something specific you can wrap your mind around. It's like they've thrown you a life preserver and are reeling you in, so you don't feel like you're floating away.

How Soon before the Actual Separation Should You Break the News?

You want to tell your child about the separation long enough before it takes place for her to start to get used to it but close enough to the actual event so that she doesn't have to go through a long, painful period of mourning as she watches her old life slipping away. Psychologists call this "anticipatory anxiety"— the anxious feeling you get waiting for something you're dreading to take place. It's often the most painful time, so you don't want the waiting to be too prolonged.

It is normal and part of the grieving process for the period of time after the children have been told and before the actual separation takes place to take on a bittersweet poignancy for both the parents and the kids. Activities that you engage in regularly become imbued with meaning:

- "This is our last Sunday morning pancake breakfast all together."

- "This is the last time we watch our favorite show all together."
- "This is the last Monday that Dad will be here when I leave to go to school."

Marking these painful milestones is part of an important process of integrating that this is really happening and a necessary step in healing. Don't be afraid to witness and acknowledge your child's sadness. You're all going through something profound, and part of being attuned is sharing it together.

A good rule of thumb for determining the best time for *the divorce talk* is to count backwards from when the parent who will be moving plans to leave. Children aged twelve and older should be told two to three weeks before the actual separation. Children who are six to twelve should be told a week to ten days before, and kids younger than six should be told about a week before.

And finally, tell them at a time when you and your spouse can be home afterward for as much time as they need to talk it through and ask questions—not, and as happened to seven-year-old Adam, when you are driving them to school. A weekend morning, when not too much planned, would be perfect. You may not need several hours at that first *telling*, but you'll want to be around and available even after they go back to their rooms.

Where to Tell the Kids

Is there a place in your house where you all typically get together to talk about things? Do the kids pile onto your bed on a Sunday morning to snuggle up and watch cartoons? Do you sometimes hang out in your son's room to talk about the events of his day? Is the breakfast table the place where the kids do homework and puzzles and play games?

Professionals often suggest that parents hold a family meeting in the living room, but unless the living room is the place you all gravitate to normally, it can feel so weird and formal that the kids will know something is wrong even before you open your mouth.

So where to tell the kids? Think about where you would talk to the kids about anything else that might be important, and do it there. We just want to avoid the awkward lineup of the kids surrounding one parent on one sofa and the other parent marooned alone on the other sofa, or any other painful configuration like that.

TAKEAWAY from *When and Where to Tell*

- Generally, it's best to tell all the kids at the same time, but there are exceptions.
- Choosing when to tell the kids is strategic. Try to avoid breaking the news while you're still in a highly volatile state, if you can.
- It's helpful if you have a clear plan of what will be happening next in terms of living arrangements.
- Calculate the best interval between *the divorce talk* and the point at which a parent moves out, based on your child's age.
- Choose a place to break the news where the family typically congregates and the kids feel comfortable.

CHAPTER 9

Honesty

One of TV's first sitcoms back in the fifties was a charming show called *I Remember Mama* that was about a Norwegian immigrant family living in San Francisco. The show was narrated from the point of view of Katrin, the eldest daughter. She told how, when she was growing up, if she needed money for school, Mama would fetch the old cigar box down from the shelf, count out the fifteen cents she needed, and then say, "Dat's goot. I'm glad I have 'nough here in the box so I don't have to go downtown to the bank to get more money."

When Katrin grew up, she learned that the few assorted coins in the old cigar box were actually all the money the family had in the world—there *was* no account in a bank downtown. However, Mama would always make it seem that there was plenty of money in the bank so that the kids wouldn't feel insecure. She understood that sometimes a parent has to soften the truth (OK, lie) in order to preserve a child's fundamental sense of safety.

This chapter on honesty and the next one on affairs and blame offer more background so that you can know how to handle the fourth of the *Seven Steps for Breaking the News* in which you decide what to say to explain why you're getting separated. One of the questions I asked the kids in the study was what advice they would give to parents who were about to tell their kids that they were getting a divorce.

Here's the gist of what many of them said:

- Annika, 3 at the time her parents divorced: "Just be honest."
- Georgina, who was 5: "Be honest."
- Sean, 15: "Be honest."
- Marie, 16: "Don't try to hide anything."
- Brad, 14: "BE HONEST"
- Jamie, 17: "Be honest as much as possible."
- Sunny, 6: "Be honest."
- Maureen, 13: "Just tell them. They can deal with it."
- Kevin, 11: "Tell your kids! Be honest!"

You get the picture: they really, *really* want you to be honest! But before you rush off to enlighten your kids about what a lyin', cheatin', womanizin', piece of doggy doo-doo their father is, listen to Karen, thirteen years old when her parents divorced, who advised, "Be honest, but not too honest." And that's why I told you about Katrin, Mama, and the old cigar box. Sometimes it's right for a caring parent to edit the facts in order to protect the kids.

Twelve-year-old Naomi's father told her solo that he would be moving out. He so very much didn't want Naomi to be upset that he lied about what was really going to happen. She recalls:

He said, "Your mother and I have been having problems in our marriage for about ten years, so I'm going to move out for a little while and live somewhere else with some friends." I asked, "Are you coming back?" and he said, "Yes, in about a year." I don't remember too much after that, as I was probably in shock. I vaguely remember my father telling me that he loved me and that it had nothing to do with me. My biggest wish was that my father would return; my biggest fear was that he wouldn't. When my father never returned to the marriage or the family, I realized the worst thing he said was that he'd be back in a year. Separating parents should not make promises they can't keep, especially to blindsided twelve year olds.

There's no doubt that kids don't want to be lied to. Most truths eventually come out, and then the child feels betrayed that you lied. That doesn't mean, however, that you can't craft *the divorce talk* strategically to protect them from damage done from knowing too much of the brutal truth. Kids want to know the truth, but they also feel strongly about something else—not being dragged into the middle of their parents' issues.

So we have a dilemma: how to tell enough of the truth without flooding your child with intimate information about the parents' relationship that, once spoken, can never be reeled back in. Here's what Joyce, who was three when her parents divorced, said: "Be as honest as you can but also, try to think about how you want your children to see the separation. What do you want them to feel and think about it when they're older? Then, be that situation as best you can. Try not to criticize the other parent. Always remember, that's your child's mother or father, and what they think of them is part of how they think of themselves."

Very wise, little Joyce! Remember how I said that we all have a right arm and a left arm, a mother and a father. You can survive if you lose the use of one of them, but do you really want to damage it on purpose?

Further to the topic of honesty, here's some other advice for you from some of the kids:

- Kendra, 13: "Try not to bad-mouth each other."
- Mikey, 5: "No hateful comments or bitterness."
- Tiffany, 8: "Don't overshare the reasons why."
- Tracy, 11: "Please keep them out of it. Don't involve them in your decision making. Don't abuse your relationship with them by telling them things you shouldn't, and, for God's sake, don't put them in the middle!"
- George, 13: "Be truthful about what is happening, but keep your own stuff out of the telling."
- Tillie, 8: "Don't bash the other parent."
- Paul, 15: "No matter how much you want to hurt your ex, DO NOT drag the children into it in any way."

Some parents use the banner of honesty as an excuse to tell kids damaging things about the other parent. They reveal all sorts of private information and then blink their eyes and innocently state, "I was only being honest." I don't buy it. When the relationship between the child and his parent is purposefully and unnecessarily damaged, it's not the other parent who pays the biggest price—it's the child who suffers.

Parents sometimes purposefully make the child feel insecure financially as a way of blaming the one who chose to leave. A father may say something like, "You know, now that your mom is leaving, we won't be able to afford to send you to ballet school anymore."

He feels he's presenting the cold, hard truth, but in reality he's destabilizing the child's sense of security. Even if it's true that they will not be able to afford ballet school after the separation, it's better to frame the situation by explaining that they are going to take a break from ballet school for a while rather than intimating that now, because of mother's selfishness, they're going to be so poor that ballet school will be out of the question.

Psychotherapist M. Gary Neuman, author of *Helping Your Kids Cope with Divorce the Sandcastles Way*, writes about parents who feel they owe their kids: "the truth, the whole truth, and nothing but the truth. These parents may embellish their announcement with detailed descriptions of the other parent's flaws and transgressions, or they may express their own uncertainty, fear, and anxiety. Often their goal is to make their children feel 'included' in the divorce. Rest assured, children need no encouragement in that direction. If anything, they need encouragement and explicit permission to disengage from parental conflicts."

Christina McGhee, author of *Parenting Apart*, suggests parents give serious consideration to what they are going to tell their children: "If you are feeling a strong desire to tell your side of the story, consider asking yourself the following questions first:

- How is this information going to help my child?
- How could this information hurt my child?

- Have I dealt with my own feelings about the situation?"

How do you balance both the need to be authentic and truthful and the need to protect your child's relationship with both parents? By using the principle of "need to know."

The Principle of Need to Know

Some of the parents I've worked with say things like this:

- "My daughter needs to know that men lie so she will be careful when she starts having boyfriends. That's why I have to tell her about her father."
- "My kids need to understand that a good mother chooses her kids before her career so they won't make the same mistake when they grow up."

In my opinion, these parents are cooking up reasons to give themselves license to tell the kids about some failing of the other parent as a way of teaching some supposed lesson for the future. In reality, that's just an excuse. These are complex issues that developed over years in the context of the parents' relationship, not black-and-white life lessons that the child really needs to learn.

There are times, however, when kids *do* need to know things in order to understand what's happening in their lives—but you must think carefully about whether sharing that information will do more harm than good. Here are some examples of things that kids actually may need to know because there is no way to avoid it:

- A parent is moving out to live with an affair partner.
- A parent is addicted to alcohol or drugs.
- A parent is suffering from mental illness.
- A parent is planning to move to another city.
- A parent has revealed that he is gay or she is a lesbian (but only if that parent wants to tell the kids).

- A parent has committed a crime and is going to jail.
- A parent has been forced to leave as a result of violence or abuse.

These events are so significant that news of them may be impossible to keep from the kids. The information is likely to seep out, and if the child learns through other sources, he may feel deceived. The best approach is for the affected parent to be open and explain to the child what's going on.

Unfortunately, however, events of this magnitude sometimes make it hard for the affected parent to be available and loving to a child because he or she is overwhelmed. In such cases, the other parent should explain the situation or else the child may feel that it's his fault that, for example, daddy left without talking to him. It's far better to explain the struggles that parent is having directly to the child. The trick is to explain in a way that is as neutral and evenhanded as possible, and to resist using that explanation as an opportunity to poison the child's view of the other parent.

Let's say that a mom is addicted to drugs and is barely functioning. Here's an example of how direct the father could be:

> Kids, I think you know that there are some things going on, and I want to clarify what's happening. Your mom has been really struggling but has not been able to stop taking some drugs that are bad for her. You've probably noticed that we've been fighting quite a bit, and that's what we've been fighting about. I've been trying to get her to agree to get help, but she's not ready. So, I think it's not a healthy environment, and I've decided that I want to separate. I hope that Mom can concentrate on getting well again. You guys will be living with me but you'll be able to visit your mom.

This may seem like a lot of information to throw at kids, but in a case like this, where a parent is unable to function, the children need to understand. Even very young children, three or four years old, need a version of this explanation if Mom is not able to take care of them properly. But notice that although the dad told his kids what was going on, he did not blame or belittle their mother.

The parent who is giving a talk like this must think carefully about how to present the news. If at all possible, the parent who will be explaining the situation should first talk it through with the addicted parent so that they can decide together what message to convey.

TAKEAWAY from *Honesty*

- Kids who participated in the study wanted honesty but needed that honesty to be tempered with protection from harm by being exposed to too much.
- The theory of need to know suggests that parents *only* reveal those details that the child really must understand.
- If it becomes necessary to reveal a parent's serious problem to the children, do so without criticism or blame.

CHAPTER 10

Affairs and Blame

Many marriages end as an immediate result of the revelation of an affair, either because the parent having the affair decides he or she wants out or because the other parent cannot tolerate or recover from the break in trust. People typically view any affair as a betrayal and just out-and-out wrong—the cavalier act of a heartless person who is only interested in his or her own self-gratification. Sometimes, however, an affair is really the desperate act of a spouse who feels profoundly lonely and rejected in the marriage. The reasons that people become involved in affairs are not always black and white, in spite of the damage that results.

Is it necessary to tell your child that you're separating because of an affair? Psychologist Robert E. Emery rightly points out that if there's been an affair, it will gall you to say that you're separating because Mom and Dad are not happy being married. On the other hand, revealing the affair to your child may turn him against the parent who strayed, perhaps forever. You'll certainly be tempted to do this if you're the injured party and want to prove that you're not to blame. But what is the value of permanently damaging your child's connection with one of his parents if the affair is over or the affair partner was not a significant person in the straying parent's life?

This is where we question the need to know. Often parents say that the child needs to know because there's a lesson to be learned—that affairs are bad and destroy families or that the kids need to know the kind of person the errant parent really is. But there's no doubt that moms or dads can be excellent, responsible, loving parents in spite of the fact that they've had an affair. Please consider whether shattering your child's trust in one parent benefits her enough to make it worthwhile.

If a parent is leaving because he has fallen in love with someone with whom he plans to build a new life right away, then definitely, the kids need to know—and *the leaver* should be the one to tell them, perhaps with the other parent in the room. Emery suggests a script that might go something like this:

> I need to tell you that a big reason why we are separating is that I have fallen in love with someone else and I'm still in love with her. This is very difficult to tell you. I'm not proud of how it happened but I wanted you to hear about it from me. Learning about all this has been very hard on Mom and this is part of the reason we have been fighting so much. This is really a grown-up problem and I'm sorry it's affecting you.

I know that telling your kids that you're having an affair is an awfully hard thing to do, but it's better than letting them find out from someone else. At the very least, you can respect yourself that you had the guts to face the situation and tell them. Please try to not be defensive or blame the other parent in this *telling*, even if that's your true feeling. Just be simple and factual. Even young children understand that the parent has done something wrong. Your kids may be very mad and lash out at you, but please don't lash back. They're only reacting that way because they're hurt.

Tina, who was eight when her parents divorced, has clear advice about introducing an affair partner to the kids: "Wait a MINIMUM of four months after you met your new partner before introducing them to your children. And integrate your partner into your children's lives, not the other way around. And do this all SLOWLY. A breakup may be all right for you, but it is devastating for a child who needs a feeling of security and stability at home."

If you are planning to move right in with the affair partner, however, *the divorce talk* is not the time to give your children too many details about him or her. If they ask, you may say that you will be moving in with someone, but explain that you would prefer not to talk about that part of what's going on right now. Some parents are so elated about their new love that they mistakenly think their kids will be happy for them. Take it from me: your kids probably won't.

As Tina suggests, the longer you can keep that part of your life separate from your kids, the better. They need time to heal from the fact of their parents' breakup before they will be ready to start integrating anyone else in their lives.

Telling the Kids Who's to Blame for the Decision to End the Marriage

A lot of parenting books suggest that you should avoid making it clear who initiated the separation, but I think this is a very tricky issue. On the one hand, your children can read you well enough to know who is the reluctant spouse. This is particularly true when one parent is deeply grieving and the other has already emotionally disconnected. To announce that you *both* have decided to separate, each of you twisting yourselves into a pretzel to present a false but unified front, may cause the children to feel confused or shut out.

On the other hand, one of our primary goals is to protect the children's relationship with both parents, and some kids will blame the parent who initiated the divorce for splitting up the family. Paradoxically, however, sometime kids blame the other parent for driving away the one who chose to leave.

My concern is for you to stay attuned with your children and have an authentic relationship, without purposefully damaging their connection with either parent. With that in mind, if you can avoid clarifying who made the decision to leave, do so. It does not have to be part of *the divorce talk* if the kids don't ask.

If the children become stuck on that point and really need to know, and if there's no way you can convincingly build a case that the decision was mutual because it's just too distant from the truth, then you can let them know who asked for the separation while carefully trying to not vilify that initiating parent. Explain who initiated the separation while, at the same time, avoid blaming that parent by simply saying something like this: "Your mom has decided that she will be happier if we live apart. I can't say I'm in agreement, but I respect her need to do what's right for her."

A statement like this one lets the kids know who asked for this separation without injecting the announcement with too much of the anger or pain you may feel about it. I know how much you want your child to sympathize with you, but it's more important to keep the child's best interest at heart, and to do that you need to permit your child to love both parents. The adult issues of the breakup should be kept between the adults. And even if you don't spell it out now, over time the truth does tend to seep out and the child may eventually learn what happened. Psychologist Anthony Wolfe suggests that you minimize the blame issue: "Don't try to deflect blame. Blame is really about feeling hurt and angry. If the kid blames you and you try to explain, they won't listen anyhow. Instead say, 'I know you blame me and you feel bad about the divorce' and leave it at that."

If, however, your kids are demanding to know, and the fact is that you've both been batting the word "divorce" back and forth and have been mutually dissatisfied with your marriage, avoid pointing the finger at the initiating parent just because he or she blinked first. Be honest! If you were considering ending the marriage but your spouse beat you to it, you don't really have cause to say that it was the other parent's decision. In that case, you will want to present the decision to your child as being more of a mutual one.

TAKEAWAY from *Affairs and Blame*

- Parents are sometimes tempted to tell the child about an affair as a way of absolving him or herself of any blame, but the damage done to the parent-child relationship may never recover.
- It's not necessary to tell the kids who initiated the separation, if they don't ask.
- If the kids need to know, tell them who asked for the separation, without demonizing that parent to the child. When one parent wants the separation and the other is totally against it, it's inauthentic to pretend that both are in agreement.

CHAPTER II

The Actual *Divorce Talk* – Parts 1-3

Have you ever sat in a doctor's office and heard some really bad news? I have. Years ago, I accompanied my husband when he was told that he had an incurable form of cancer and had about three months to live (which turned out to be a misdiagnosis). As soon as the doctor said, "I'm sorry to have to tell you that you have cancer," the air was sucked from the room and my mind jammed: "What! What did he just say?" I replayed the tape to make sure I got it right. Meanwhile, the doctor went on talking about test results and possible treatments. I saw his mouth move but all I heard was noise, because my mind had locked on the words "You have cancer."

I wanted to ask, "Did you just say that he has incurable cancer?" "Are you sure?" "Is it definite?" "How could that be?" I wanted to stay with those first three words, "You have cancer," trying to keep them from skittering off my brain. I was struggling to integrate the fact that my world had just shifted on its axis and nothing was ever going to be the same. As a result, anything the doctor was saying was meaningless. I couldn't take it in. This chapter and the next will explore the fifth of the *Seven Steps for Breaking the News*—the actual telling.

Daniele, a mother who consulted with me, described how she was planning to tell ten-year-old Anya about the upcoming separation. First, she planned to say that Mom and Dad were having troubles and that she was moving out, but it was OK because

Anya could help decorate her new room and would go back and forth, one week with Mom and one week with Dad, so she would see lots of each parent, and they would always be there for her, and they loved her, and it wasn't her fault.

Whew! This loving, worried mom wanted to make the upcoming changes seem as benign as possible. No doubt, however, Anya would have been overwhelmed by all that information at one time. I coached Daniele to tell the first piece of information (Mom and Dad have been having some troubles) and then to step back and give Anya time to digest that cookie before going on to the next.

Many children feel overwhelmed because they really don't understand what they've been told. Let's face it, even the adults are pretty confused right around now and often don't have a clear picture of what's coming next, so it's understandable that the kids are confused too. But, because of this confusion, children may fill in the blanks with awful fears about the future. Listen to the panic in the words of six-year-old Tyler as he wrote about it a few years later: "I was really stress too cause i knew that something bad was hapening to my family. I was afraid to leave with my mother cause i was afraid to sleep outside on the walkway! It was not realis but . . . i was 6 so . . . Abandon, lost , i was cryin. Didnt know what really happening . . . They didnt explain us really was it was. It was like chosse the one you love the most and you will never see the other again! I wanted to go with my mother but didnt know that she had a place to live . . . i was thinking that we had to sleep outside on the walkway!"

Poor Tyler was not given a clear picture of what was to come, so he was fearful about whether the separation meant that he might not even have a home! Many of the kids in the study were confused about the concrete plans. They didn't really know what separation or divorce means, and even if they were teens, they really needed things spelled out for them.

Marianne, another mom I worked with, told me that she felt she'd done it well. Her ex had been too depressed to tell six year-old Jenna and continually delayed the inevitable. Finally Marianne said, "We can't wait any longer. I have to tell her." She told Jenna solo. She carefully explained that they were separating and simply said, "We'll be much better friends if we were living apart."

Jenna cried a lot, but Marianne didn't try to make her feel better. She just held her and said, "Yes, it's awful," until Jenna stopped crying. Marianne was able to tolerate Jenna's sadness because of her conviction that she would eventually get over it— or maybe, if not over it, at least around it.

Marianne's approach demonstrates the cornerstone of *the divorce talk* that we've been talking about—attunement. She was attuned to Jenna's needs and, by so being, was able to make that painful event in her daughter's life a bit less distressing. Marianne accepted her ex-husband's need not to be present during the telling. In this case, it was too much for him and it was wise to do the telling without him there but with his agreement.

The divorce talk is a six-part process that ideally is more of a conversation than an announcement. The primary purpose is to get the message across that the parents will be separating and to help the child with his emotions. That's essential. If you can also provide some information about plans for the changes coming up, that's good but secondary. Although the six parts are described here as an orderly sequential roll out of information, in reality, *the divorce talk* will twist and turn, some parts coming before others, some becoming primary and others either not being addressed or mentioned in only a sentence or two.

Be careful not to flood your children with too much information at this first revelation. There is a two-step process that takes place when a highly emotional event occurs. First you have to make space for all the feelings to be expressed, and only when the emotions have been adequately tended to can the brain absorb new information. I will discuss this concept in detail in the chapter on the attuned response.

So here we go. You've decided who will speak and what you want to tell your kids. You've been repeating your mantra in your mind to make sure that you're as centered as possible under the circumstances—in your best adult, loving, parental mind space. You've poured some steel in your spine. The family is together in a comfortable place, and the kids are cuddled up close to a parent, dog, cat, grandpa's blanket, or whatever is comforting for them and the room is nice and warm. Both parents are going to be around the house for a good period of time after *the divorce talk* because your child will need you. If the two of you are at war, you've signed a temporary truce so that you can nail this thing and do it as right as possible—knowing that it might turn out to be a mess, but at least you really tried!

The Six Part Process

The six part *the divorce talk* outlines an ideal scenario. Please don't feel you've failed if, for whatever reason, you're unable to give your child the calm, adult, attentive, attuned rollout of the revelation. You're trying your best at a difficult moment. Your child may storm out of the room and refuse to talk to you. You may lose your temper at your spouse or child and say something you'll wish you hadn't. You may cry too much or sit in stony silence. Please give yourself love and know that you can do some repair work later. You're only human!

Sixteen-year-old Tamar's advice to parents is simple and direct: "Don't try to make it better than it actually is. Tell all the truth right away, making sure to have agreed on the living conditions of the children. The very first thought after processing THEIR divorce is 'What about me?'"

She's right. Most children's primary concern is, "But what's going to happen to me? Am I safe?" Some children worry, "Will my mom and dad be OK?" Depending on their age, they may also need to know, "Why is this happening? Whose fault is it?" and "How could you permit this to happen?" And finally, "What's going to happen next? Who will move out and when? Will we have to move? What's going to happen to the cat?"

Part One—Preparation

Part One sets the stage to help your children anticipate that the news might not be good. People hate bad surprises, so if they can recognize that something is coming, even a few moments before the revelation, they'll feel somewhat less sideswiped than if the first thing you do is blurt out the news that you're getting divorced.

Introduce the fact that things have not been good with Mom and Dad, or that one of you feels that things have not been good. Spend some time exploring the kids' awareness that there are problems. How much did they have a sense that something was wrong? If the problems were obvious, what did they think about it?

Here are some opening things you can say:

- "Have you guys noticed that we've been fighting a lot lately?"
- "Mommy and I have been having some serious talks about our marriage recently."
- "I didn't understand why, but your dad's been so quiet lately. I thought it was because of work, but it's more than that. He told me that he's been very unhappy in our marriage."
- "Remember when we took separate vacations this summer and we told you it was because of our schedule? Well, it was more because we've been having a hard time being together recently."

If your hyperaware kids twig right away where this conversation is going and ask, "Are you guys getting divorced?" then don't prolong the agony. Launch right into Part Two!

Part Two—The Revelation

It's important to make sure your kids really understand what's going on. Unfortunately, as psychologist Joan B. Kelly writes, this doesn't always happen: "Most kids were not adequately explained about what is going on. When parents provided an explanation, it was brief and failed to explain how the separation would affect their lives. Children were therefore left to struggle alone with the meaning of this dramatic event, exacerbating feelings of isolation and cognitive and emotional confusion. Parents were most likely to just reassure kids that everything would be fine, especially the parent who sought the divorce."

Tell them that there's going to be some changes in the family and Mom and Dad will be living separately. If you tried hard to find a solution or went to marriage counseling, let them know. Notice that the examples below don't use the word "divorce"; instead, they use "separation." That's intentional, because separation comes first, so it's more accurate.

Use words that are simple and honest—don't sugarcoat! Psychologist Robert E. Emery says: "Candy coating the situation may buy you some time, but at a high price: your children's trust."

That said, you don't want to explain the intimate details that led to the marriage's breakdown. The complexity of what happened cannot be explained in a few sentences, and whatever you say will stick in your child's mind forever. He will ruminate on those words, and they will become a burden to him. And truly, there are things that happen in a couple that are adult matters and not appropriate for sharing with a child or teen.

As I've noted earlier, it's preferable for both parents to participate in *the divorce talk*, each adding a bit more information. The few sentences that are the backbone of it could be similar to the following, with modifications that suit your particular situation. Here are some things you can say:

- "We want you to know that some things are going to be changing in our family."
- "We've been fighting so much that living together isn't any fun anymore."
- "Your dad and I have been struggling with this, but try as we may, we can't find a way to stay together happily. We've decided to separate."
- "If we could have found a way to work it out, we would have because our family is so important to both of us."
- "We are deeply, deeply sad and sorry that our relationship has come to this point."
- "We know this is shocking news and that you're really upset to hear it."
- "We love you both so much and hate having to hurt you, but we're going to work very hard to make this as easy as possible."
- "We want to hear all your feelings, now and in the future."
- "Getting used to the changes will be hard, but you will. You won't always feel this badly."
- "We love you and we will all always be your family, but it will be a family with two homes instead of just one."

As these examples illustrate, there's a fine line between providing your child with an explanation that will help him understand ("We just don't feel happy being together anymore") and an explanation that may detonate in his mind ("After Trisha was born, your mom just got all wrapped up with you kids and forgot I existed").

A child can understand that two people are not happy together. You don't have to give a reason for that. Once you've opened the Trisha squiggly can of worms, the children are likely to become engaged in assessing who's right and how it happened, and maybe even start to blame Trisha. It's too much information and yet not enough for any person to really understand—which your child cannot and should not. Explanations similar to the ones above give your child something to hang on to without burdening him with distracting and disturbing details.

Part Three—The Emotional Response of the Child

Help your kids express their feelings about this news, both verbally and nonverbally. Give them time. Sit in silence with them as it sinks in, or give them the OK to be mad, to cry, or even to run out of the room. Again, the chapter on the attuned response will give you all the tools you need to handle all of your children's emotions.

Some children are reserved and not forthcoming in expressing feelings. They don't like talking and easily feel awkward and exposed. You want to gently encourage them to share what they are going through; but if they're not willing, back off and respect their wish for privacy. They may look unaffected, which may make you feel relieved, but that nonchalant appearance masks a lot of feelings inside that they may be suppressing.

Quiet, mature pre-adolescent Stephanie writes about the toll it all took on her: "I think it is important for people to realize that just because a child might look like they are handling the situation very well, doesn't mean that they are. I was like the little soldier at twelve, marching on along as though nothing had happened, comforting my mom. There were no visible signs of how traumatized I really was inside."

Be careful to keep a watchful eye on kids who appear unaffected. Notice changes in mood or behavior, and check in with them from time to time, asking, "What're you thinking about all this stuff about Daddy and me separating?" If they shut you down and say something like, "Nothing. Everything's fine," you can't force them to open up. What you can do, however, is to be sure to spend more time with them and try to connect in other ways. Make a point to be around, talking about other, less sensitive, issues. Spending time together, even if you are not talking about it, can be reassuring to your children.

About those kids who react minimally or with apparent indifference to the news, psychologist Anthony Wolfe writes: "How does he feel about it? He's very upset. That's how he feels about it. He probably doesn't feel like talking about it because he would burst into tears, which he apparently doesn't want to do, and his parents must respect this. Parents should let their kids react however they want and need to react."

Kids who are impulsive and angry may raise the stakes and make wild declarations guaranteed to upset you (e.g., "I'm not living with either of you! I'm moving out!" or "You're doing this on purpose to ruin my life!" or "I hate you and I'll never speak to you again!"). Sometimes this is a powerful bid to get you to change your mind. The child is demonstrating to the nth degree how outraged he is and is hoping that the intensity of his pain will force you to back down.

When this happens, you need to be calm and straightforward, but don't back down. If you hesitate, the child will sense it and up the ante, making matters worse. Respond to the feelings behind your child's words and although you need to take note of the content, focus on the driving emotion behind it.

Rather than taking the bait ("You're not moving out. You're only seventeen, and where do you think you're going to go?") and getting into a debate, address the feeling behind that declaration ("I know that right now you wish you could get far away from all this and not have to deal.").

Rather than taking the bait ("Don't get dramatic. Your life isn't ruined!"), address the feeling ("I know it must feel like nothing will ever be the same, and that's an awful feeling.").

Rather than taking the bait ("Don't you dare say you hate me. This is no picnic for me either, young lady!"), address the feeling ("Of course you hate us right now. That's normal when someone has made a decision that changes your life without consulting you."). Divorce therapist M. Gary Neuman wrote, "You don't have to rescue your child from his feelings, and you don't have to defend the events and behaviors that led to your decision."

Focusing on the feelings rather than on the content lowers the temperature and relays a message to your child that you can accept his anger. It's normal. This is just the very beginning of a journey for your family. You need to be strong and tolerate whatever rises to the surface at this very early stage. Ride the wave and don't be too reactive.

TAKEAWAY from *The Actual Divorce Talk – Parts 1-3*

- As soon as your child understands that what you're telling her is that you're getting separated, a whole emotional reaction will be triggered, making it hard for her to focus on anything else you subsequently say.
- You need to connect with your child's emotions before you can provide information. Don't overwhelm your child with too much on the first telling.
- *The Divorce Talk* is a six-part process. The first three parts are:
    - Preparation—Raise the issue that there are serious problems in the parents' relationship.
    - Revelation—Give enough of an explanation without flooding the child with too many details as to why you are separating.
    - The child's emotional response—Make space for the child to express whatever he needs to say.

CHAPTER 12

The Actual *Divorce Talk* – Parts 4-6

This chapter continues the explanation of the six-part process of *the divorce talk*.

Part Four—The Parents' Response

Offer an attuned response to your children's reactions with patience, understanding, and reassurance. Notice that you're not refuting their emotions, just echoing them, and not trying to cheer them up. You're giving them permission to feel whatever it may be that they are feeling.

You or your spouse may get emotional, tear up, or cry. That's OK, but try to keep these expressions of your own emotions within limits, because the focus should be on the kids' emotions. If you're too wrapped up in your own grief, you're going to lose sight of them.

Odette, who was nine at the time, describes how her parents were able to both be emotional and make her feel secure at the same time: "I think they were both careful and focused on me. I don't remember clearly, but I expect my mother cried in a careful 'I'm sad, because this is sad, but it is really OK, and everything is still under control' sort of way. I don't remember my father's reactions at all, but I expect they were fairly stoic and gentle, with his full attention on me. Certainly their full attention was on my emotional state and reaction."

Give your child space and time to react, and don't be freaked out if that reaction is powerful. Remember that sobbing, trembling, or shaking is the body's natural mechanism for using up the adrenaline produced when there's been a shock. Don't interrupt it—it will run its course if you don't get in the way. It's a good thing that the child is letting out those feelings—much better than burying them. More on this in the next chapter on reducing the risk of trauma.

Here are some things you could say:

- "You're mad! Of course, you're mad! This is the last thing you wanted to hear!"
- "It's OK to be mad. It's normal! A big change is taking place. You don't want it and you don't have any say about it."
- "It's fine to cry. This is really sad. Let it out! Let out all your feelings. Cry as much as you want!"
- "Don't worry about hurting our feelings—we need to know what you're going through right now."
- "I know you have a lot of feelings inside and that sometimes it's hard to let them out. That's understandable. If you want to tell us even a little bit of what you're feeling, we'd be happy to hear."

You can use art material or puppets to help younger children express their feelings. For example, you can use a puppet to say what you imagine your child may be feeling: "L'il Lamb is saying, 'I don't want Daddy to move out! That makes me very, very sad!'" Give your child another puppet and ask, "I wonder what kitty cat is saying?" Then you can have a conversation, using the puppets to help your child talk it out. Often it's easier for small children to use puppets to express themselves than it is for them to talk to their parents directly.

Another tool you can use is to give her some drawing paper and markers and tell her, "Draw me a picture of what you feel inside!" Let her scribble in black or draw furiously as much as she wants. It is very therapeutic. She can tell you what the drawing means or not – her choice.

Part Five — Concrete Plans and Information

If you already know the details of when and where one of you will be moving, you may want to be prepared with some photos of the new place, should your child be in the frame of mind to take a look. Lynn Lyons, psychotherapist and specialist in childhood anxiety, suggests that with younger kids, it can help to draw a picture of Mom's place, Dad's place, and the road that connects them. The concrete diagram of what life will be like later helps the child grasp what the changes will mean.

How much this initial discussion includes specifics really depends on the climate in the room. Kids who were expecting the separation may have already done quite a bit of the preparatory emotional work and are ready to move on to the next phase and want to hear the details. You have to use your judgment as to whether it's wise to spell it all out. Will it help or hurt for your children to hear, "You're going to be with Mom from Wednesday to Saturday and with me from Sunday to Tuesday, and you'll have month in the summer with each of us"?

If you don't really know the details yet, or if there is tension between you about how the separation is going to play out, please do not bring that into this initial discussion. Instead, say, "We're still in the planning stage, so we don't have any specifics to tell you right now. We'll let you know as soon as things get ironed out, but not to worry! You will with have a home with both of us!"

Part Six — Q&A

It is important to check to make sure that your child understands what you've just explained. You can ask her to repeat back what she's just heard. Take your time and stay with this until you're confident that she gets it. Very young children will probably need you to explain what separation means many times over the coming days and weeks until they can grasp all the aspects. As a start, you can simply explain that you will always be their mommy and daddy but will be living in two different homes, and they will stay with each of you (if that's true) part of the time.

Ask for and answer questions, no matter how strange they may seem, and take all their concerns seriously. Sometimes the first things children worry about seem odd or trivial, like who's going to drive them to swimming practice or will they still go to the birthday party on Sunday. Be patient and invite any questions that are on their mind.

These kinds of questions test how normal your child's life is going to be after today. Answer with a few words, and avoid a long explanation or a lecture. Remember, his ability to process what you're saying may be limited at this point. Be brief, for now.

As mentioned earlier, kids may ask if you're getting a divorce. It's best to just keep this first discussion centered on the fact that you're getting separated, unless an actual divorce is imminent. That way, the child can adjust in stages. It's normal for a child to hold out hopes that you'll change your mind, and some kids wage a campaign to that effect. Even if you know it's set in stone that divorce is next, give your child a few weeks to get used to the idea before sharing that information, but don't give false hopes. It's kinder to say that the decision to separate has been made and is definite, even if your child (and you) don't want it to be true.

Another level of questioning may arise. Your child may ask things like, "Are you having an affair?" or "Is mommy leaving because you never pay any attention to her?" or "Are you leaving because Mom spends more time with Grandma than she does with you?" You need to prepare an explanation for the separation that is understandable to your child but doesn't draw him into private and intimate detail. Participants in the study said they want simple reasons, without too much detail, such as these:

- "You've seen us fighting."
- "We can't be happy living together."
- "We are not getting along, but it's not your fault."
- "We can't work out our differences."
- "We love you and want you to grow up in a happy atmosphere."

It's acceptable to draw a veil of secrecy around the real reasons for the separation if knowing the truth would be damaging to your child. You can say, "What's been going on between us is really an adult issue and, as much as we want to help you understand, we've decided to keep it private."

The Meta Message

Ideally, here is the message behind the message. Everything you say should be imbued with it:

- "We love you."
- "Our separation is not your fault (even if we fought about you)."
- "We will try our best to have a good, workable relationship."
- "You are free to love both of us."
- "You did not do something to make this happen."
- "We will not put you in the middle."
- "Life will eventually return to normal, but it will be a new normal."

A therapist friend of mind, Pat Love, told me about the Buddhist principle that life is 10,000 joys and 10,000 sorrows. No one makes it through life without facing sorrows. The separation of parents in a family is one of them. But the key is what you do with that reality and, most importantly, how you use it as an opportunity to show your child how to face life. You may wish never to suffer or for your child never to suffer, but that's impossible, so you'll have to find an accepting place to position that suffering. To be really enlightened is to welcome joys and sorrows equally—they mean that we're alive.

Trauma specialist Peter A. Levine writes: "I have come to the conclusion that human beings are born with an innate capacity to triumph over trauma. I believe not only that trauma is curable, but that the healing process can be a catalyst for profound awakening—a portal opening to emotional and genuine spiritual transformation."

When you permit your child to express her sorrow or anger rather than scrambling to cheer her up, you're demonstrating that we don't need to run from it. We need to make room for all aspects of life. We know that sorrow comes, then things evolve and the sorrow softens and we're into the next part of life. That's true for your child and true for you too. If you try to run away from emotional pain, it gets stronger. You know how scary it feels to run away from something. But, if you accept it as part of living, it becomes more benign.

TAKEAWAY from *The Actual Divorce Talk* – Parts 4-6

- *The Divorce Talk* is a six-part process. The last three parts are:
  - The parents' response—Keep the focus on the child's reaction. You may use art material to help him express himself.
  - Concrete plans and information—It helps some kids to know specifically what will be changing in their lives but you have to gauge whether now is the time to tell.
  - Q & A—Check to make sure your child understands and expect that he may ask some odd questions as he grappling with the news.
- The Meta message: You can't avoid suffering in life, so it's best to learn how to accept it and not run away from it.

CHAPTER 13

Reducing the Risk of Trauma

Teddy was nine when his parents separated. Before the separation, their explosive relationship was evident for all to see. The fights, doors slamming, cursing, threats of divorce, instances of one leaving the house and then the other were an all-too-real part of family life. Teddy, an only child, was anguished about it all and would routinely make them promise that they wouldn't get a divorce. They'd comply, not knowing what else to do, postponing the inevitable—until the time came when it was impossible for the marriage to continue. Teddy's father was having an affair, and his mother was furious. She told him, "You did this. You tell him."

Teddy's tears started the moment his father asked him to come into the living room for a talk. Even before the words left his father's mouth, Teddy had thrown himself on the floor, kicking, screaming, and—most painfully—begging, "Say you won't get divorced! Say you won't get divorced! Say you won't get divorced!" He was inconsolable and in such a hysterical state that after about ten minutes, his father once again backed down and said, "OK. We won't." That was a lie. His parents did get divorced, and Teddy was furious for a very long time.

In this chapter and the next, we will talk about the sixth of the *Seven Steps for Breaking the News*—how to be attuned to your child's emotions in order to reduce the risk of trauma during *the divorce talk*. You often hear that divorce is traumatic for kids, but people are usually referring to the experience of growing up with divorced parents. One of the unexpected results of the study that led to this book was the realization that *the divorce talk* itself may result in an actual clinically diagnosable traumatic response, similar to what a child might experience from being in an automobile accident.

Individuals are at risk of experiencing emotional trauma when they learn something they perceive to threaten their lives or security. At the moment of hearing some profoundly disturbing news, whether it has to do with the illness of a beloved grandparent, the death of a pet, or the possibility that their parents might separate, some kids have such a strong fear reaction that their bodies respond physically, kicking into protective mode. The need to protect the body's integrity stimulates the amygdala, the part of the brain entrusted with keeping us safe, releasing adrenaline. The primitive amygdala is unable to discriminate between an actual threat, such as an attacking dog, and an imagined threat, like the unknown life changes that accompany parental separation.

Were he attacked by a real dog, your child would need all the tools his body could muster in order to run fast, freeze, jump a fence, or do whatever it would take to protect himself. Adrenaline would be shot into the bloodstream, triggering a series of instantaneous physiological changes that stimulate the heart, circulatory system, and muscles so that he could react strongly. By the time the actual physical crisis passes, the adrenaline has done its job of propelling the body to respond and has been used up, allowing the nervous system to calm down.

When a child experiences a *perceived* threat, however, the fear he feels stimulates that same protective reaction so, although he is sitting quietly in your living room, his heart may be racing, his vision darkened, and all the blood in his stomach may be rushing to his legs, preparing him to run. But, because his body doesn't really need to physically protect itself, he gets stuck with all the preparatory physiological changes with no way to discharge all that energy. As a result, he feels awful—sweaty, nauseous, shaky, with a sense of the world being distant and strange. And it's weird and scary.

He's completely wrapped up with trying to cope with the alien feelings in his body and can't comprehend the actual meaning of what he's heard. He only knows that whatever it is, it's bad. He doesn't understand what is going on, and that makes him feel helpless. He needs you to first address his physical and emotional state before he'll be ready to take in more information. Until he has had time to work through his initial shock, he simply won't be ready to think about the practical side of things. This is crucial!

In *Trauma through a Child's Eyes*, Peter A. Levine and Maggie Klein write: "Trauma happens when any experience stuns us like a bolt out of the blue; it overwhelms us, leaving us altered and disconnected from our bodies. Any coping mechanisms we may have had are undermined, and we feel utterly helpless and hopeless. It is as if our legs are knocked out from under us."

Here are some responses from kids in the study when asked what they felt when they were told:

- Jonah, 13: "Just numb emotionally."
- Samantha, 8: "I was in a state of shock. I did not know how to process the idea. I don't think I felt anything at the time. I didn't really understand what was happening."
- Kay, 13: "I panicked. Devastated. It was the end of life for me. I cried and died inside. I felt dead."
- Bridget, 12: "I can look back now and say I was in shock."
- Tiffany, 12: "I was totally overwhelmed. I was totally shocked."
- Amanda, 10, overheard her parents arguing when she was in bed: "My parents did not know I was awake and listening to their conversation in the other room—guess they thought I was still asleep. After my father left the house to go to work, I got out of bed and went into the kitchen to

confront my mother, but nothing came out of my mouth.
I was crying and shaking and at this point she didn't know
I had overheard what was discussed between them and
started shaking me to speak and asking what was wrong
with me. I was paralyzed in speech. Finally, still sobbing, I
was able to get the words out that I heard the conversation.
I was extremely shocked and that day, that conversation
changed my life and it would never be the same again."

- And most heartbreakingly eloquent from Veronica, who
  was 7: "A series of losses loomed up in a huge, overwhelming way that I can only describe as completely, utterly huge.
  I remember feeling totally alone. I remember being on a
  high stool and observing my tears just plunking onto the
  ground in a most dramatic and oversized way. I am not sure
  if my mother left the room, but if she didn't, I certainly re-
  ceived no warmth or support. No questions were asked for.
  I remember thinking, 'I am losing everything—my bedroom,
  my dolls, my hallway, my house, my cousins, my school.
  I am going to lose it all.'"

Veronica describes a sense of total alienation and despair. Her
description of her reaction suggests that she experienced some
degree of dissociation—a way of distancing from reality that is
one of the mechanisms that help trauma survivors cope. She was
all alone on a high stool, observing her oversized tears falling to
the ground, as if in a dream. She imagined that her parents' news
meant the loss of everything secure and valued—home, school,
family, even her dolls. To sum it up, here is Peter A. Levine and
Maggie Klein again: "Trauma is about loss of connection—to
ourselves, to our bodies, to our families, to others, and to the
world around us."

It's easy to recognize that fear of loss of connection in Veronica's words. Regrettably, Veronica's parents didn't know what
she was thinking and feeling. Had they been attuned and available to her, this traumatic experience could have been avoided.

What Causes the Traumatic Reaction?

Now that we know that children may experience trauma when they learn about their parents' divorce, how do we reduce the risk? If we look at what causes the amygdala to fire, causing the fight-or-flight response that leads to all these intense physical symptoms, we can identify that it's fear. So we need to track backward and figure out how to reduce the risk of fear. What causes fear in this situation? I think two factors are at work.

First, the word "divorce" has tremendous power. We live in a culture where divorce is universally acknowledged to be bad. It's a given that no one wants it, and it is used as a metaphor for something painful, like going to the dentist and paying taxes, only worse. You can't watch television for an hour without coming across a negative depiction of divorce. A good divorce is a rarity, and even very young children know that. Often, when parents tell a child that they are getting separated, the first question the child, with trembling voice, will ask is, "But are you getting a divorce?" The message is clear: separation is bad, but divorce is worse.

The word "divorce" signals two things: conflict and loss. Sadly, a marriage breakdown brings out the worst in people, so it's not uncommon for divorced parents to have high-conflict relationships. Kids' lives are too often rigidly split between two households. As a result, they may go days without seeing, or even speaking to one parent or the other. Moreover, witnessing the conflict and anger between the two people they love and depend on most hurts deeply.

But it doesn't have to be this way. I once worked with a divorced family in which the parents had remained friends. They lived in the same neighborhood, so during the weeks when the kids were with the mother, the father would drive them to school every morning and vice versa. That way, the kids had time with both parents every day. These kids had an excellent post-divorce situation because there was no tension between the parents. But this situation is rare, and it's not what most kids expect when they hear about their parents' plans.

The second feature that leads to fear during *the divorce talk* is the fragile emotional state of one or both of the parents. The act of telling the kids about the divorce stresses the parents so much that the kids sense that something awful is about to happen, which leads to the fear response. Obviously, this telling shatters the dream of the happy family, and once the words have been spoken, the fact of divorce has morphed from possible to real.

An emotionally fragile parent is very scary for kids. Kids depend on their parents to be strong and stable enough to protect them, and a parent who is distraught and so wrapped up in her own world that she's unable to provide the emotional support her child needs, triggers a powerful reaction of fear of loss of connection.

You cannot change all the messages your child has digested about how divorce sucks, but you *can* help her see that there are more positive ways of handling a divorce and reassure her that you will strive to accomplish that. And you can work to manage your emotions so that, even though you may be sad or angry, you are rooted in your role as a parent who can take care of her.

Reducing the Risk of Trauma

Peter A. Levine and Maggie Kline strongly encourage parents to adopt a calm demeanor to help a child at risk of experiencing trauma. They write that it is not primarily through words that parents transmit the message that the child will be OK; rather, it's through body language, facial expression, and tone of voice. I'm sure you know that. But what do you do when you are so upset or even traumatized that you can't disguise your body language?

The answer is to just do your best. If you are aware of needing to pull it together, and you make the effort to get out of your bathrobe and get dressed, wash your tear-stained face, comb your tousled hair, and present your best face for the sake of your child at *the telling*, you'll be showing your child that you haven't fallen apart.

If you carefully craft *the divorce talk* so that you don't succumb to the temptation to use it as a tool to get your child on your side, and you make a solemn pledge to yourself that, at least while you're in front of your children, you'll keep your language clean and will not, under any circumstances, deteriorate into a bitter conflict with their other parent, then you're ahead of the game. And even if you tear up and cry, or your voice wavers, or you look sad or mad, as long you have enough self-control to take the high road, then you've done a good thing for your child, my friend, and you can pat yourself on the back.

Now is the time for you to reach down and pull up your best stuff, your most mature self, your adult persona, and let it shine. I know it's not easy. But I know you can do it!

Creating a Trauma-Reducing Environment

Several years ago, a woman suffering from mental illness attacked me on the sidewalk. She chased me down the street, and when I tripped and fell face-first on the pavement, she leaped on my back, choking me from behind. Some passersby, one of whom had been walking her German shepherd, pulled the woman off of me. As I sat on the sidewalk, waiting for an ambulance (I'd broken my foot), I asked the dog owner if I could hold on to her dog. I put my arms around him and held him close until the paramedics arrived. I always credited that dog as the reason I was not traumatized by the attack. The dog showed up just at the moment that I needed comforting, and hugging him did the trick.

Physical contact calms the nervous system. No matter how old your children are, please make physical contact with them when you have your talk (unless, of course, they make it clear that they don't want you to touch them). Little kids should be on your lap. Come equipped with a blanket to keep them warm or a stuffed animal to cuddle. If your kids are older, hold their hands or put your arm around them. Get your dog or cat on board. If your children will permit you to give them physical comfort, please do. It's also best if *both* parents can be in close physical proximity to the kids.

Stay emotionally connected as well, no matter what your child is going through. Just be there. You need to accompany him emotionally to resolve the physiological state of trauma he may have entered into. Your child's body will need to discharge all its pent-up, residual survival energy. This may come out in the form of fighting, yelling, sobbing, shaking, or sitting as if frozen in place. Most importantly, stay close and calm and trust that your child's body is doing what's necessary to work through this first emotional shock. Simply assure him that his feelings are normal and he's going to be OK.

Children who participated in the study emphasized how important it was to them that their parents reassured them that they would try to keep life as normal as possible. You can't make impossible promises, but acknowledging and addressing your child's fear of change will help to minimize that fear. One way to do that is to explain exactly what will change and what will stay the same after the separation. In the last chapter, I suggest an exercise in which you make a chart outlining *What Will Change and What Will Stay the Same*. Making these changes concrete, and signaling that a lot of things will remain the same, is comforting for your child.

TAKEAWAY from *Reducing the Risk of Trauma*

- This study indicates that some children experience an actual clinical trauma when they learn about their parents' impending separation. Their body's protective mechanism kicks into a fight, flight, or freeze response, making them feel very weird and scared.
- Children become traumatized when they feel alone, alienated, confused, and unsupported.
- Trauma occurs as a result of the fear of conflict and loss.
- Parents can reduce the risk of a traumatic reaction by presenting a calm, adult demeanor at *the divorce talk.*
- Staying in close physical and emotional contact with the child helps to reduce the risk of trauma.
- Provide a lot of reassurance that you will work hard to keep things as normal as possible.

CHAPTER 14

The Attuned Response

When I first started my practice as a family therapist, one of my first passions was parent education. It would break my heart when families would come in with angry teens who desperately wanted their parents to understand them, but by the time the kids were fifteen or sixteen, the gulf between the generations was miles wide. The parents loved their kids, and the kids wanted to be loved—but the kids sure didn't feel as though their parents "got" them. I decided to focus on doing "preventive medicine" and started offering parenting courses based on the classic parenting book *How to Talk So Kids Will Listen & Listen So Kids Will Talk* by Adele Faber and Elaine Mazlish.

Parenting 101

There's a lot to learn about parenting, and I'm now going to give you a crash course that's based on material from that book. The basic idea behind developing what I've been calling "attunement" is for parents to listen carefully, acknowledge and accept their child's reality without trying to correct it or change it. Much of what children express, even in everyday things, makes us anxious. Your seven-year-old daughter says she hates her teacher, your ten-year-old son says his best friend is stupid, and we don't like to hear it.

We worry that if she hates her teacher she won't do well in school. If he calls his friend stupid, he'll get into a fight. There are a lot of feelings behind those statements, but we're focused on the possible negative outcome, so we try to change our children's thinking. When your daughter says she hates her teacher, you may react with, "Don't say that! Ms. Gleason is a very nice woman!" And when your son says his friend is stupid, you may retort, "You're going to end up with no friends at all if you say things like that!"

The problem with our normal knee-jerk response is that we are not really listening to what our child is trying to say—and he knows that. He feels frustrated with us and, over time, stops trying share his feelings with us. He shuts down, and then later you show up at my office with a sullen teen who in no way is going to open up to you.

Parenting 101 teaches us to be attuned to our child's feelings—listening carefully, acknowledging and accepting. When he feels really heard, he *wants* to have a deeper, richer discussion with you and *wants* to invite you to help with what's on his mind.

You accomplish this by reflecting back to the child the *feeling* behind the words *without trying to change it*. When your daughter says she hates her teacher and you say, "Don't say that!" the conversation ends there—with her now not only hating her teacher but also annoyed with you! But, if instead, you responded with, "You're not having a good time in class these days" (a simple reflection or repetition of what your daughter said) she will be more likely to continue with, "Yeah, Ms. Gleason made me read in front of the class today and I felt bad 'cause I made so many mistakes."

Now you're getting the richer, deeper story. And if you can just stay with the feelings and say, "You didn't like that," then your daughter may continue with, "I was feeling all hot and I almost started to cry." If you can continue to stay with her, without trying to cheer her up, and say, "That's an awful feeling," she can go on with her story or not. Although she had a rough time in class, at least she feels that you understand—that you are attuned to and accept her feelings—and that is enough to make her feel better.

You can't go back in time and stop what happened in Ms. Gleason's class, but you can help your daughter feel that you understand her and that she's not alone. And we know, as adults, that what we all yearn for is to feel completely understood and not alone.

What's wrong with trying to cheer your child up? The answer is simple: she needs to tell her full story and let her feelings come tumbling out, and it's annoying to have to be cheered up. We sometimes *want* to hang on to our bad feelings for a while. We need to follow them through to the end, until they peter out and we naturally start to feel better.

Learn to Tolerate the Full Range of Your Child's Emotions

Staying with the bad feelings and making space for your child to tell you all about them is counterintuitive. It makes parents anxious. We fear that if we let our child talk too much about things that upset her, she'll feel that we are agreeing with her and become even more upset—but the opposite is usually true. Paradoxically, when a child has permission to express her bad feelings, she'll be more likely to get enough distance from them to work through them, and gradually those bad feelings will start to soften.

Think about it from an adult point of view. Let's say someone upsets you at work. You want to share the story with a close friend and tell all aspects of it so you can impress upon your friend the intensity of the injustice done to you. If, after a sentence or two, your friend says, "Don't get so worked up about this—it's not so bad!" in a genuine bid to cheer you up, you're likely to feel frustrated and answer with, "Yes, it is bad. You don't understand what it was like! It was awful!" Then you will try harder to convince your friend how bad it was, maybe even by exaggerating the awfulness.

Imagine that, instead, your friend just listened quietly and paid close attention to the entire story and, after you were finished, said, "Wow! That sucks!" Chances are that you would feel good that you had been understood. Your friend can't make that awful scene at work not have happened, but at least you have the satisfaction of someone validating your reality. And that, as they say, is priceless.

Resolving an emotional hurt is a two-step process. You can't engage the logical brain until the emotions come out. Think about how easy it is to react irrationally when you're upset by something. In the example above, you might have said, "That's it! I'm quitting that job!" Making that declaration sure feels good. It feels like you're taking action, even though you know you don't mean it. Once you've had the chance to tell your story and the emotions have been released, you'll look at the event in a different way and will probably change your mind about quitting. Put another way, the two steps to resolving emotional hurt involve first releasing emotions and then engaging logic:

- *Emotions.* Let the emotions wash over you, unmediated by reason, and find a way to express those emotions so that they will be heard and validated.
- *Logic.* Once the emotions have run their course, your logical brain will naturally kick in to make choices that are in your best interest.

Sandra L. Bloom, M.D., wrote: "When stressed, we cannot think clearly, we cannot consider the long range consequences of our behavior, we cannot weigh all of the possible options before making a decision, we cannot take the time to obtain all the necessary information that goes into making good decisions. Our decisions tend to be based on impulse and are based on an experienced need to self-protect."

Riding the Emotional Storm

Due to the changes taking place in your life, you're probably pretty emotionally depleted and don't have a lot of energy left to work on a graduate degree in parenting. I promise that what I'm suggesting is actually quite easy once you get the hang of it. You can't avoid emotional pain so you might as well learn how to not only tolerate it but also accept it as part of being alive. That's true for you, and it's true for your child. In other words, since there's no way around it, you have to go through it.

An attuned response means:

- Being straightforward and as honest as appropriate when doing *the divorce talk*
- Watching and listening carefully to your child's reactions
- Answering questions simply and truthfully, taking into account the emotions behind your child's question
- Reflecting back to your child what you believe to be his *feelings* at the moment
- Continuing to reflect back and to restate his feelings, giving him room for his emotions, no matter what form they may take
- Hanging in there, without trying to sugarcoat the situation or cheer him up
- Toughening up, pouring some steel in your spine, and learning to tolerate the emotions
- Not running away, either emotionally or physically, but instead waiting until your child's emotions have run their course

You'll be surprised how powerful an attuned response is toward soothing your child even if it doesn't appear to be working right away. You'll know you have honored those emotions enough when your child changes the subject and asks, for example, "What's for dinner?"

At the start of the previous chapter, we learned about Teddy, who became hysterical when he sensed that his parents were getting a divorce. How could Teddy's parents have handled his powerful reaction more effectively? What can parents do to be attuned to their children when confronted with a similar reaction?

- Acknowledge your child's feelings from the moment the first tears well up in his eyes: "You're worried about what we have to tell you."
- When he throws himself sobbing on the floor, state his reality: "You've lived through so much watching your dad and me struggling in our marriage, and you very much don't want us to separate."
- State what you can see he's feeling: "This feels like the worst thing that could possibly happen to you."
- When he begs you to promise that you won't get divorced, acknowledge what he's feeling: "You wish with all of your heart that we won't get separated."
- Get down on the floor next to him. Try to pat his back or gently hold his ankle. If he doesn't want you to touch him, just sit beside him and don't get up until he does.
- You don't even need to talk, other than to confirm what he is saying.
- Don't try to cheer him up. Just being there is enough.

You're demonstrating that you can tolerate his pain and that you don't need him to cheer up or make it better. Avoid superficial reassurances such as, "Honey, you'll see. It's going to be fun having two homes!" Statements like this do more for the parents who make them than they do for their child. Oddly, showing that your child's pain is not overwhelming to you will make it less overwhelming to him. You don't need to say it—you're showing it energetically by being next to him.

Notice that everything you say should be totally focused on your child and his emotions. You shouldn't be trying to justify your actions or explaining what will be happening, and you shouldn't tell him that he'll feel better later. Instead, you're in the moment with your child and his strong emotions—and I have to tell you, it's the right thing to do and a great gift you can give him.

You're saying to him, "Yes! Yes! This is awful! This is bad! And you have a right to feel that way." And, miraculously, the more you're in tune with him and his emotions, the sooner they will start to recede. Once the emotions have been spent, he'll be able to think about other aspects of what is going on.

Bear in mind, however, that Teddy may take a long time to get to that point. It's not going to happen in a day. He has witnessed a lot and there have been many times that his parents lied to him to try to avoid his distress. There will be a long period of working through, but these parents need to give him this time. And most of all they need to not be afraid to tell him the truth about his reality so that he can regain trust.

Your child may tell you that he hates you, but don't take it personally. At that moment, he probably does hate you. Sometimes kids tell their parents that they hate them, but then they feel badly about it. You can respond with, "I know you hate us right now, and I also know you love us. Hate is just an emotion and sometimes comes even when you love someone. It's OK."

We've now learned that to soften the risk of trauma, it's important for the child to not feel alone. Through using an attuned response, you are connecting to what your child is feeling and saying, and you are not protecting yourself from your own fear of where those feelings might lead. You're getting your own ego out of the discussion so that you can connect freely with your child, starting with where he's at. Remember: your ears should be bigger than your mouth!

TAKEAWAY from *The Attuned Response*

- Parents often get anxious when faced with their child's strong negative emotions and react by trying to avoid or eliminate that expression.
- Parents need to be able to tolerate intense anger, sadness, and emotional pain and give their child the opportunity to express his full range of feelings. When a child is free to express himself, it is easier for his feelings to naturally resolve.
- The emotions have to come out before the logic can kick in.
- An attuned response means accepting your child's emotions and acknowledging the *feelings* rather than immediately responding to the content of what he's saying.
- Your child will feel closer to you if you are appropriately tuned in.

CHAPTER 15

Strategies for Staying Attuned after the *Divorce Talk*

So, now you've crossed the bridge and arrived in the new land—you've told the kids. I hope it went better than you'd feared. Even if it didn't, at least you can take pride in knowing that you tried to do it well. You did some reading, you thought about what and how and where to tell, you tried to tame your own inner emotions and rise above. Please give yourself some love for all you've tried to do to protect your children.

Here we will be talking about the last of the *Seven Steps for Breaking the News*—following through so you can remain attuned. This is, of course, just the start of a transition that will evolve very slowly over a long time. Continuing to help your child after *the divorce talk* means two things: (1) staying connected to your child's emotions and reacting with attunement and, in most cases, (2) fashioning a workable co-parenting relationship with your soon-to-be former spouse not only for your child but for yourself as well. You don't want to live an extended part of your life in conflict with someone with whom you need to do as delicate a job as raising a child together.

Strategies for Helping Your Child Talk about It

Roberto, who was three when his parents separated, advises parents that *the divorce talk* should be an ongoing conversation. He said, "Keep talking to them. Don't have a conversation once and then consider the matter 'discussed.' Kids need time to adjust and consider and think and their perspectives shift with time. It's so important to come back and talk things through again and again. Let the child do some talking. Give them space to question, to be angry, to be sad. Be as honest as you can but also, try to think about how you want your children to see the separation. What do you want them to feel and think about it when they are older? Then, be that situation as best you can."

Your child's reaction *will* shift and change over time. At *the divorce talk*, he may react one way, but as reality sinks in and he has a chance to think it through, it's normal that other feelings will surface. Staying in touch with him in the days and weeks following the revelation can mean using the direct approach of asking, "Hey, how're you doing with all this?" However, many kids don't like talking, don't know how to put all of their confused feelings into words, or (bravely) don't want to upset their parents by telling them how lousy they feel.

It may be hard to break the ice and begin a conversation on this topic, so here are some conversation starters to help you get your kids talking about the separation or divorce. It's always best to ask open-ended questions rather than ones that invite a one-word answer. If, for example, you ask, "How're you doing?" you may not get much more of an answer than "Fine." Try one of these instead and see if it opens doors:

- "It's been a week since Daddy moved out, and I was wondering what it's been like for you to not have him living here with us."
- "We only had one conversation about why we separated, and I'm not sure we were clear enough. Why do you think we separated? How have you explained it to your friends?"
- "I was listening to the radio the other day and I heard a kid talking about what it was like for him when his parents got separated and I started thinking, I wonder what it was like for you?"

- "Sometimes when parents break up, it's pretty confusing and kids get lost in the shuffle. What's on your mind that you'd like me to know?"
- "I know you're really busy with your own life, but I just thought I'd check in with you and see how you're doing with all the changes since we separated."
- "You're probably wondering about some things. What would you like to know about the divorce?"
- "I got this book about kids and divorce. Let's look at it together."
- "I guess you might have some feelings about the divorce that are hard to talk about, so I got these worksheets we can do together."

Sometimes it helps to use creative ways of expressing feelings. You can spend time together with art material and puppets. This is a great way for kids to open up about their feelings either non-verbally or indirectly. You can make a "feelings board" together (like a vision board but for feelings). Get a bunch of magazines, a glue stick, markers, poster board, and glitter (why not?) and help your child cut out pictures and make a poster of how she's feeling. If it's pretty grim, maybe suggest she make a second one to show how she hopes to be feeling later, when everything settles down.

Some kids are comforted by have a clear picture (literally) of the changes to come. You can draw a visual map together, if you know the location of the departing parent's new home. "Here's Mom's house on Melrose Street, here's Dad's house on Northcliffe Avenue, here's Grandma and Grandpa's house, where they always are on Argyle Road, and here's your school. Here's the road between our two houses." Then together, decorate the map with trees and flowers and cars driving back and forth between Melrose and Northcliffe.

Along the same lines as the visual map, you can work with your child to make a chart called *What Will Change and What*

Will Stay the Same. This visual description can also be very comforting for some kids. Take a piece of poster board and draw a
vertical line down the middle. Label the left side *What Will
Change* and the right side *What Will Stay the Same.* Then think
of all sorts of items to complete both sides. Make some of them
funny; for example, under *Stay the Same* you might write "Daddy
will still always park too far from the curb" and "Jennifer will
sneak treats to Bongo the dog under the table thinking no one is
noticing."

For kids who like to write, you can provide them with a new
journal or diary and a special pen and encourage them to spill out
all their feelings. Writing is an excellent way of healing. Tell your
child to write it *all* down, even or especially the bad stuff. Suggest that they write a story or a poem that describes what it's like
for them. They can keep it private or share it with you if they
want.

Gary Sprague, author of *Kids Caught in the Middle: An Interactive Workbook for Teens* suggests helping kids express their
feelings by circling words for the various emotions they're feeling. I like that type of tool—some kids find it easier to circle a
word than to have to say it out loud. If your child connects with
this, you may suggest that he circle the words every few days or
once a week and compare how his reactions are developing.

Here's Sprague's list of descriptive feeling words. You can add
whatever you think is right for your child.

Angry	Loved	Scared
Afraid	Depressed	Grieving
Confused	Hopeless	Mad
Happy	Shocked	Relieved
Lost	Guilty	Lonely
Sad	Rejected	Worried
Glad	Helpless	Sorry for myself

Technology also offers some brilliant ways for kids to express themselves. I once conducted an entire therapy session with an angry ten-year-old boy without either of us saying a word. He very much didn't want to be in my office and made it clear he was not going to talk, so I grabbed my laptop, opened a blank page, and wrote, "Hi! My name is Vikki. What's yours?" Then, I passed him the computer. He typed in his name and passed it back. The ice was broken and we had a very meaningful digital conversation, without his having to go back on his promise that he would not talk during the session. With pre-teens and teens, a lot can be accomplished with texting!

Some parents used books and music to help their kids with the emotions, and I highly recommend that you be prepared with some books that are appropriate for your child's age.

- Maggie, 3 years old, said: "My mom was very attentive and just held me until I felt better. I remember she played a *Sesame Street* record for me."
- Jasmine, 10, wrote: "Mom gave me the book, *A Smart Girl's Guide to her Parents' Divorce* by American Girl."
- Risa, 5, said: "What helped was reassurance from Mom and reading *Love You Forever* by Robert Munch."

You can also stay connected with and comfort kids who are less expressive by just spending extra time together, throwing a ball around, going ice-skating, or hanging out at the library. You don't really need to talk about "*it*" for the child to know that you're there for her. The purpose of all these strategies is to make sure your child knows you care about her feelings and to prevent her from feeling bottled up inside.

Of course, try as you might, some kids are just not going to come out from behind the wall. They don't want to talk, draw, or make things with a glue stick or hockey stick or any other kind of stick. They don't want to allow their parents the comfort of comforting them. That may be their way of punishing their parents, or maybe it just comes from some mixed-up, angry place inside that they can't set right, even though they may want to.

Please don't be discouraged or vindictive. Being a kid is hard enough without complications. Please be patient and continue to be available without pushing it. And, if there's anyone else who connects with this child—a family friend or relative—concoct some reason for that person to spend time with him.

Finally, under strategies to help your child express herself, you can suggest she complete the questionnaire that I prepared for kids and teens in order to research this book. It's available at the back of the book. Working on the questionnaire and talking about it with you will open up a rich conversation about what it was like for your child. And you may want to complete the questionnaire for parents.

Creating a Functional Co-Parenting Relationship

Gabrielle was ten when her parents divorced. There's pride in her voice as she describes the ideal scenario her parents created for her and her brother:

> My mother wanted to make sure the lines of communication remained open, so she'd have little touch-points and just make sure we were OK and didn't need to talk about things. Both parents never (I mean NEVER) spoke badly about the other to us, either initially or later after time had passed; this was a sure strength in the whole equation and transition! It was too bad that it had to happen, but I still feel that not only the day they told us but all those after, my parents had the 'ideal divorce.' They were positive, my father was always plugged in, they regularly showed they cared, and you could tell they always would put us both first.

Gabrielle's parents were able to work together in what sounds like a low-stress relationship that benefitted their kids. I know that, as ideal as that sounds, post-divorce relationships such as theirs are not always possible. Often one partner is too angry or hurt and can't get past those feelings. Our culture has a lot of tolerance for bad behavior between divorced parents, but I would like to ask you to try, if you possibly can, to find ways to tamp down the ongoing conflict around the kids rather than ramping it up.

The best predictor of a healthy adjustment of children following divorce is a high level of cooperation between the parents. The hallmarks of co-parenting, as Gabrielle's parents demonstrate, are:

- Parents behave civilly to each other in front of the kids.
- Parents foster the child's relationship with the other parent.
- Each parent keeps the other informed about the day-to-day life of the child.
- Parents help each other out if one has an occasional scheduling conflict.
- Parents respect the rules at the other parent's home.
- Each parent supports the child's relationship with the other parent's family.
- Parents don't speak badly about the other parent in front of the kids.

If you were able to have a planning meeting and succeeded in telling your kids about the separation together, you've already started co-parenting. As time goes on, if you remain committed, it gets easier. There are many excellent books about how to co-parent successfully (see the recommended books at the back of this book). I encourage you to read some.

Your relationship with your child's other parent will typically continue, in one form or another, for a lifetime. When your child is still living at home, you may have to engage with your former spouse on a weekly, or even daily, basis. You've worked hard to make *the divorce talk* as smooth and non-traumatic as possible. I know you can try to keep up that momentum into the future.

The last word goes to Jacob, who was eight when his parents separated. He is now in his thirties and offers you sage advice and a possible vision for the future:

> Tell your kids that you love them. Tell them that you plan on working through the issues you have so that you can parent them together. Explain to them, as best you can, how the logistics of things are going to work out. One of the things that I am most grateful for is that my parents had a pretty amicable divorce. There was very little fighting between the two of them. As time has gone by and they have become grandparents, they have also become friends. This Christmas, I had both of my parents together for the first time in 20 years. My dad and his new wife and my mom were all together for Christmas. It was a little strange for me but it was really good.

I'm wishing you courage, strength and a lot of luck on this journey going forward. Best case scenario, you will be able to depend on your children's other parent to help you raise them, and you will encourage each other in the struggles of parenting and celebrate your children's triumphs together.

TAKEAWAY from *Staying Attuned After the Divorce Talk*

- It's important to keep connected with your child even after *the divorce talk*.
- This chapter provides many creative examples of ways to connect with your child.
- *The divorce talk* is the first step in a new relationship with your spouse as co-parents. It is important that you embrace a commitment to try to make that relationship work.

Appendix A

Questionnaire for Adults Whose Parents Divorced When They Were Children or Teens

1 How old are you now and how old were you when you learned that your parents were separating?
2 Are you male or female?
3 Were you expecting that your parents' marriage might end or did it come as a surprise?
4 Had they been fighting a lot? Was there tension between them?
5 Who told you that they were separating?
6 If you have siblings, were you all told about the separation at the same time?
7 Where were you when you were told (e.g. in the kitchen, in the car)? What were the circumstances?
8 How long was the whole conversation?
9 What were you told? What were the exact words that were used?
10 If it was your parent or parents who told you, what was their emotional state?
11 If they were both there, how did they relate to each other?
12 How did you feel when you heard?
13 What did you say or do? What did you need to know?
14 What did you and your other family members do after you were told?

15 Did you understand what was happening?

16 Did you understand the reason why they were separating? What was it?

17 Did you blame one of your parents or side with one of them?

18 Did the revelation take place soon after or before any other event, such as a vacation, camp or a birthday, which you associate it with?

19 How long after you were told did one of your parents move out?

20 What was your biggest worry, fear or wish?

21 Did your parents say or do anything that made you feel better during that conversation?

22 Did they say or do anything that made you feel worse?

23 After that first day, did you talk about it more with your parents? In what ways?

24 How do you feel now when you think about that day?

25 What advice do you have for parents who are going to tell their kids that they are separating?

26 Anything else you want to add?

Appendix B

Questionnaire for Children Up to Age 13

1 How old are you now and how old were you when you heard that your parents were separating?
2 Are you a boy or a girl?
3 Did you know that your parents might separate or did it come as a surprise?
4 Were your parents fighting a lot or very angry with each other before they separated?
5 Who told you about the separation?
6 If you have a brother or sister, was everyone told at the same time?
7 Where were you when they told you (for example, in the kitchen, in the car) and what was happening?
8 How long did they talk to you?
9 What were you told? Do you remember what words they used to tell you?
10 Did your parents seem sad, angry, calm or something else when they told you?
11 If both of your parents were there, how did they act with each other?
12 How did you feel when you heard?
13 What did you say or do?
14 What did you and your other family members do after you were told?

15 Did you understand what was happening?

16 Did you understand the reason why they were separating? What was it?

17 Did you blame one of your parents or feel sorry for one of them?

18 Did they tell you soon after or before any other event in your life, such as a vacation, camp or a birthday?

19 How long after you were told did one of your parents move out?

20 What were you most worried about?

21 What was your biggest wish?

22 Did your parents say or do anything that made you feel better?

23 Did they say or do anything that made you feel worse?

24 After that first day, did you talk about it more with your parents? In what ways?

25 How do you feel now when you think about that day?

26 Do you have any suggestions for parents who are going to tell their kids that they are separating?

27 Anything else you want to say?

Appendix C

Questionnaire for Teens

1 How old are you now and how old were you when you heard that your parents were separating?
2 Are you a boy or a girl?
3 Were you expecting that your parents' marriage might end or did it come as a surprise?
4 Had your parents been fighting a lot or obviously tense with each other?
5 Who told you about the separation?
6 If you have a brother or sister, was everyone told at the same time?
7 Where were you when they told you (for example, in the kitchen, in the car) and what was happening?
8 How long did the conversation take?
9 What were you told? What were the exact words that were used?
10 Did your parents seem sad or angry or calm or something else when they told you?
11 If both of your parents were there, how did they act with each other?
12 How did you feel when you heard?
13 What did you say or do? What did you need to know?
14 What did you and your other family members do after you were told?

15 Did you understand what was happening?

16 Did you understand the reason why they were separating? What was it?

17 Did you blame one of your parents or feel protective of one of them?

18 Did they tell you soon after or before any other event in your life, such as a vacation, camp or a birthday?

19 How long after you were told did one of your parents move out?

20 What was your biggest worry, fear or wish?

21 Did your parents say or do anything that made you feel better during that conversation?

22 Did they say or do anything that made you feel worse?

23 After that first day, did you talk about it more with your parents? In what ways?

24 How do you feel now when you think about that day?

25 What advice do you have for parents who are going to tell their kids that they are separating?

26 Anything else you want to add?

Appendix D

Questionnaire for Parents Who Have Already Told their Children About the Separation

1 Are you a dad or a mom?
2 How many children do you have (indicate boys or girls) and how old were they when the separation took place?
3 How long ago did the separation take place?
4 Was the decision to separate joint or was it solely the wish of one of you? Which one?
5 How long did you know that the marriage was ending prior to informing your child(ren)?
6 Did the two of you plan how and what you were going to say? If so, what type of planning did you do?
7 Had you planned the logistics of the separation prior to the time the child(ren) were told (e.g. who was going to move out and when, where the kids were going to live, etc.)?
8 Who was there when the child(ren) were told? If both of you were there, what was the role each of you took in the telling?
9 What was said? What were the exact words used in the telling?
10 Where were you and your spouse and the child(ren)? Was contact made with your child(ren) during the telling (e.g. them sitting on your lap, you giving hugs)?

11 What were you both feeling and showing emotionally during the revelation? How did you manage your emotions?
12 What was the emotional response of the child(ren)?
13 What did the child(ren) say or ask? What were their main concerns?
14 Did it go better or worse than you expected?
15 What did you do that you're proud of related to how the kid(s) were told?
16 What did you wish you'd done differently in the telling?
17 What advice do you have for parents who will be telling their kids that they are separating?
18 Is there anything else you'd like to add about informing the kid(s)?

Recommended Reading
for Parents

Emery, Robert E. *The Truth about Children and Divorce.*
New York: Plume, 2006.

Faber, Adele, and Elaine Mazlish. *How to Talk So Kids Will
Listen & Listen So Kids Will Talk.* New York: Simon &
Schuster, Inc., 2012.

Gaies, Jeremy S., and James B. Morris. *Mindful Co-parenting:
A Child-Friendly Path through Divorce.* CreateSpace
Independent Publishing Platform, 2014.

Lansky, Vicky. *Divorce Book for Parents.* Minnetonka, MN:
Book Peddlers, 2005.

Levine, Peter A., and Maggie Kline. *Trauma through a Child's
Eyes: Awakening the Ordinary Miracle of Healing.*
Berkeley, CA: North Atlantic Books, 2007.

Levine, Peter A., and Maggie Kline. *Trauma-Proofing Your
Kids: A Parents' Guide for Instilling Confidence, Joy and
Resilience.* Berkeley, CA: North Atlantic Books, 2008.

Lippman, Jessica, and Paddy Greenwall Lewis. *Divorcing with
Children: Expert Answers to Tough Questions from Parents
and Children.* Westport, CT: Praeger, 2008.

Long, Nicholas, and Rex Forehand. *Making Divorce Easier on Your Child: 50 Effective Way to Help Children Adjust.* New York: Contemporary Books, 2002.

McGhee, Christina. *Parenting Apart: How Separated and Divorced Parents Can Raise Happy and Secure Kids.* New York: Berkley Books, 2010.

Neuman, M. Gary. *Helping Your Kids Cope with Divorce The Sandcastles Way.* With the assistance of Patricia Romanowski. New York: Random House. 1999.

Pedro-Carroll, JoAnne. *Putting Children First: Proven Parenting Strategies for Helping Children Thrive through Divorce.* New York: Avery/Penguin, 2010.

Thayer, Elizabeth S., and Jeffrey Zimmerman. *The Co-Parenting Survival Guide.* Oakland, CA: New Harbinger Publications, 2001.

Wolf, Anthony E. *Why Did You Have to Get a Divorce? And When Can I Get a Hamster?: A Guide to Parenting through Divorce.* New York: Noonday Press. 1998.

Bibliography

Afifi, Tamara D., Tara McManus, Susan Hutchinson, and Birgitta Baker. "Inappropriate Parental Divorce Disclosures, the Factors that Prompt them, and Their Impact on Parents' and Adolescents' Well-Being." *Communication Monographs* 74 (2007): 78–102.

Beyer, Roberta and Kent Winchester. *Speaking of Divorce: How to Talk with Your Kids and Help Them Cope.* Minneapolis, MN: Free Spirit Publishing, 2001.

Bloom, Sandra L. "Trauma Theory Abbreviated." *Final Action Plan: A Coordinated Community Response to Family Violence*, Attorney General of Pennsylvania's Family Violence Task Force, October, 1999.

Burns, Alisa, and Rosemary Dunlop. "'How Did You Feel About It?' Children's Feelings about Their Parents' Divorce at the Time and Three and Ten Years Later." *Journal of Divorce & Remarriage* 31, no. 3–4 (1999): 19–36.

Cushman, Donald P., and Dudley D. Cahn. "A Study of Communicative Realignment between Parents and Children following the Parents' Decision to Seek a Divorce." *Communication Research Reports* 3 (1986): 80–85.

Ducibella, John S. "Consideration of the Impact of How Children Are Informed of Their Parents' Divorce Decision: A Review of the Literature." *Journal of Divorce & Remarriage* 24, no. 3–4 (1995): 121–141.

Ducibella John S. "An Investigation into the Effects of How Children Are Informed of Their Parents' Divorce Process Decisions." PhD thesis, Florida State University, 1995.

Emery, Robert E. *The Truth about Children and Divorce*. New York: Plume, 2006.

Faber, Adele, and Elaine Mazlish. *How to Talk So Kids Will Listen & Listen So Kids Will Talk*. New York: Simon & Schuster, Inc., 2012.

Favaro, Peter J. *Smart Parenting During and After Divorce*. New York: McGraw Hill, 2009.

Fayerweather Street School. *The Kids' Book of Divorce: By, For & About Kids*. Edited by Eric Rofes. New York: Vintage Books, 1982.

Gottman, John Mordechai, Lynn Fainsilber Katz, and Carole Hooven. *Meta-Emotion: How Families Communicate Emotionally*. Hillsdale, NJ: Lawrence Erlbaum Associates, 1997.

Grollman, Earl A., and Sharon Grollman. "How to Tell Children about Divorce." *Journal of Clinical Child Psychology* 6, no. 2 (1977): 35–37.

Gumina, Joseph M. "Communication of the Decision to Divorce: A Retrospective Qualitative Study." *Journal of Divorce & Remarriage* 50, no. 3 (2009): 220–232.

Jones-Soderman, Jill, and Allison Quattrocchi. *How to Talk to Your Children about Divorce*. Scottsdale, AZ: Family Mediation Center Publishing Co., 2006.

Kelly, Joan B. "Talking with Your Children about Separation and Divorce: Some Ideas and Tips to Help You Do It Right." CBC television. *Doc Zone*. 2012. www.cbc.ca/doczone/features/talking-with-your-children-about-divorce-some-ideas-and-tips-to-help-you-do

Kelly, Joan B., and Mary Kay Kisthardt. "Helping Parents Tell Their Children about Separation and Divorce: Social Science Frameworks and the Lawyer's Counseling Responsibility." *Journal of the American Academy of Matrimonial Lawyers* 22, no. 2 (2009): 315–334.

Lansky, Vicky. *Divorce Book for Parents*. Minnetonka, MN: Book Peddlers, 2005.

Levine, Peter A. *Healing Trauma: A Pioneering Program for Restoring the Wisdom of Your Body.* Boulder, CO: Sounds True, 2005.

Levine, Peter A., and Maggie Kline. *Trauma through a Child's Eyes: Awakening the Ordinary Miracle of Healing.* Berkeley, CA: North Atlantic Books, 2007.

Levine, Peter A., and Maggie Kline. *Trauma-Proofing Your Kids: A Parents' Guide for Instilling Confidence, Joy and Resilience.* Berkeley, CA: North Atlantic Books, 2008.

Lippman, Jessica, and Paddy Greenwall Lewis. *Divorcing with Children: Expert Answers to Tough Questions from Parents and Children.* Westport, CT: Praeger, 2008.

Long, Nicholas, and Rex Forehand. *Making Divorce Easier on Your Child: 50 Effective Way to Help Children Adjust.* New York: Contemporary Books, 2002.

McGhee, Christina. *Parenting Apart: How Separated and Divorced Parents Can Raise Happy and Secure Kids.* New York: Berkley Books, 2010.

McKay, Dean. "The Trauma of Divorce: Reducing the Impact of Separation on Children." American Academy of Experts in Traumatic Stress (1997). Accessed 10, 2013. http://www.aaets.org/article18.htm.

McKay, Matthew, Peter D. Rogers, Joan Blades, and Richard Gosse. *The Divorce Book: A Practical and Compassionate Guide.* Oakland, CA: New Harbinger Publications, 1999.

McManus, Tara G., and Jon Nussbaum. "Ambiguous Divorce-Related Communication, Relational Closeness, Relational Satisfaction, and Communication Satisfaction." *Western Journal of Communication* 75, no. 5: (October–December 2011): 500–522.

Neuman, M. Gary. *Helping Your Kids Cope with Divorce The Sandcastles Way.* With the assistance of Patricia Romanowski. New York: Random House. 1999.

Pedro-Carroll, JoAnne. *Putting Children First: Proven Parenting Strategies for Helping Children Thrive through Divorce.* New York: Avery/Penguin, 2010.

Schwartz, Lita Linzer. "Children's Perception of Divorce." *The American Journal of Family Therapy* 20, no. 4 (1992): 324–332.

Sprague, Gary. *Kids Caught in the Middle: An Interactive Workbook for Teens*. With Randy Petersen. Nashville, TN: Thomas Nelson Publishers, 1993.

Sviggum, Greta. "How Children View Their Parents' Divorce." *Family Matters*, no. 55 (Autumn 2000): 62–67.

Thiessen, Irmgard. "The Impact of Divorce on Children." *Early Child Development and Care* 96, no. 1 (1993): 19–26.

Thayer, Elizabeth S., and Jeffrey Zimmerman. *The Co-Parenting Survival Guide*. Oakland, CA: New Harbinger Publications, 2001.

Thomas, Candice E., Melanie Booth Butterfield, and Steve Booth Butterfield. "Perceptions of Deception, Divorce Disclosures, and Communication Satisfaction with Parents." *Western Journal of Communication* 59, no. 3 (1995): 228–245.

Wallerstein, Judith S., and Sandra Blakeslee. *What about the Kids: Raising Your Children Before, During, and After Divorce*. New York: Hyperion. 2004.

Westberg, Heather, Thorana S. Nelson, and Kathleen W. Percy. "Disclosure of Divorce Plans to Children: What the Children Have to Say." *Contemporary Family Therapy* 24, no. 4 (December 2002): 525–542.

Wilson, Reid, and Lynn Lyons. *Anxious Kids, Anxious Parents: 7 Ways to Stop the Worry Cycle and Raise Courageous & Independent Children*. Deerfield Beach, FL: Health Communications, Inc., 2013.

Wolf, Anthony E. *Why Did You Have to Get a Divorce? And When Can I Get a Hamster?: A Guide to Parenting through Divorce*. New York: Noonday Press. 1998.